GIVE HIM TO THE ANGELS

THE STORY OF HARRY GREB

JAMES R. FAIR

Summersdale Publishers
46 West Street
Chichester
West Sussex
PO19 1RP

A CIP catalogue record for this book is available from the British Library.

ISBN 1 84024 011 3

Printed and bound by Biddles Ltd, Guildford and Kings Lynn.

Other books and videos by Geoff Thompson:

Watch my Back - *A Bouncer's story.*
Bouncer (the sequel to *Watch My Back*).
The Pavement Arena - *adapting combat martial arts to the street.*
Real Self Defence.
Real Grappling.
Real Punching.
Real kicking.
Weight Training - *For the Martial Artist.*
Animal Day - *Pressure testing the martial arts.*
The Tuxedo Warrior - *Tales of a Mancunian bouncer.*
By Cliff Twemlow. Foreword By Geoff Thompson.
Fear - *the friend of exceptional people.* (Techniques in controlling fear.)
Blue Blood on the Mat.
By Athol Oakley. Foreword Geoff Thompson.
On the Door - *Further Bouncer adventures.*

The Ground Fighting series:
Vol One - Pins, the bedrock.
Vol Two - Escapes.
Vol Three - Chokes and Strangles.
Vol Four - Arm Bars and Locks.
Vol Five - Fighting From neutral knees.
Vol Six - Fighting From Your Back.

Videos - (all videos one hour approx)
Lessons with Geoff Thompson
Animal Day - *pressure testing the martial arts.*
Three Second Fighter - *the sniper option.*
Throws and Takedowns vol 1-6.
Real Punching vol 1-3.
The Ground Fighting series (videos):
Vol One - Pins, the bedrock.
Vol Two - Escapes.
Vol Three - Chokes and strangles
Vol Four - Bars and joint locks.
Vol Five - Fighting from neutral knees.
Vol Six - Fighting from your knees.

About the author:

Geoff Thompson is one of the most recognised martial arts figures of this century with some twenty bestselling books on the contemporary role of martial art to his name and is currently the BBC Good Morning self defence expert. He has taught his unique method of self protection to the police, the Royal Marine Commandos, in local government, on Excel Body Guard training camps and also on the professional circuit. He has worked in training camps for professional world class boxers advising on fear management and in-fighting techniques. Geoff writes regular columns for several publications including: SG's Martial Arts Plus, Martial Arts Illustrated, Combat, Traditional Karate, Fighters, Terry O'Neill's Fighting Arts International, Muscle Mag (Britain-USA), Black Belt Magazine (USA), Fighters (Sweden) and Australasian Fighting Arts (Australia). He has also featured in mainstream glossy magazines such as Loaded, Maxim, Esquire and has published several articles with GQ Magazine (Britain-Paris). Geoff is qualified in innumerable systems of combat. He is a presently a Sambo Russian Wrestling coach, Olympic Greco Roman Wrestling Coach (FILA), Olympic Free style National Wrestling Coach (FILA) Judo Coach, Ju-Jitsu Coach, British Combat Association Coach, EKGB 4th Dan, JKA 2nd Dan, Shaolin Modga gung fu 1st Dan, ABA assistant Boxing coach, and BTBC Muay Thai boxing coach. He is a former UK weapons champion and is trained in the use of the Defensive Flashlight and the PR24 Side Handled Baton and is affiliated to ASLET (American Society for Law Inforcement Trainers) He has also studied Aikido and weapons.

Geoff worked as a night club doorman for nine years in some of the countries roughest nightspots, graphically re-lived in his autobiographical bestselling books Watch My Back, Bouncer and On The Door, and travels the country teaching realistic self protection and combat stress management to some of the country's top martial arts practitioners.

FOR MY WIFE SHARON, AS ALWAYS,
WITH ALL MY LOVE.

TO MUM AND DAD, I LOVE YOU VERY MUCH.
THANKS FOR 37 YEARS OF TOTAL SUPPORT AND
ENCOURAGMENT

Introduction

A short time after publication of For Whom the Bell Tolls, Bill Corum, the New York sports columnist and radio announcer, was interviewing Ernest Hemingway at the Stork Club. It apparently was just a routine interview until, suddenly, Hemingway opened up on a well-known writer who once had interviewed him at Bill Browne's health camp.

"Why that fellow," he thundered, "didn't seem to know anything. There was Browne telling him some of the greatest stories I ever heard about Harry Greb, and he didn't know who Greb was....Imagine a man not knowing one of our great Americans !"

For quotes, I wanted to know why Hemingway considered Greb a great American, so I wrote him. Getting no reply, I concluded that either he didn't get my letter, or that, having gone to Europe as a Collier's correspondent, he decided the war was more important than Harry Greb.

There was only one thing to do and that was to consult Whitey Bimstein, who is not only the world's most famous handler of prizefighters, as well as a double-talk and hot-foot-giving artist, but also a figure in the international social set. Didn't he sit in the royal box with King Alfonso at the San Sebastian bull fights ten years ago when, at the king's request, he went to Spain to handle Paolino Uzcudun, the Basque Woodchopper, against Primo Carnera, the Varicose Venetian? While the effervescent, gold-toothed, battle-scarred heavyweight champion of all the Spaniards was elbowing Mr. Bimstein in the ribs and nodding in the direction of a curvacious, slinky, olive-skinned senorita, Alfonso, with an obvious eye on diplomatic Washington, remarked that he was fond of Americans. A tactful man himself, Mr. Bimstein returned the compliment. Pointing a long, hairy finger at the cutie, he wowed Alfonso when he said, "There's nuttin' wrong with the Spaniards, either, king. Some built!"

Mr. Bimstein was in what he calls his chambers at Stillman's gymnasium, naked save for a towel slung around his middle. He was kneading the muscles of Joe Baksi, his current heavyweight sensation, who was stretched out on the rubbing table. Jammed into his chambers, a locker room about the size of a Chic Sale two-holer, was an assortment of Runyon characters. They were firing questions at Mr. Bimstein, who was answering them with a degree of finality of which only he is capable. If you think it doesn't take a man of substance to have the final say with Runyon characters, drop in at Stillman's before two o'clock any afternoon and observe the Harry the Horses in session.

Mr. Bimstein's sharp blue eyes picked me up as I gently threaded my way past these men.

"Hot !" he said half-heartedly as if he wasn't sure it was. It was so hot the top of my head felt like a slab of molten lead.

He summoned Coco, who doubles in brass as his assistant and as court jester to the king, same being Mr. Bimstein. Coco is maybe a little short of five feet; a frolicsome hunk of rotundity who can shake a passable shimmy when the king demands it and whose last name no one seems to know.

"Take over," Mr. Bimstein commanded, slapping Mr. Baksi in the slats and fading away so Coco could come in and finish the musclekneading.

I told him about my one-way correspondence with Hemingway.

"He don't reply?" Mr. Bimstein asked incredulously.

"No, but maybe he didn't get my letter," I said, not wanting to put the onus on Hemingway. "On the other hand, maybe he figures Greb is underneath the war." (Underneath is a term Stillmanites use instead of saying their man is working in a preliminary to the main attraction.)

Mr. Bimstein burped on a hotdog he was washing down with a growler of beer and rubbed his stubbly white beard. ""Hemingway'll find out different," he snapped.

Chapter I

Angel with a Busted Beak

There couldn't have been a better title for the story of Harry Greb than Never Call Retreat. Actually, it isn't true to say he never retreated. No fighter with a brain in his head or with a view to keeping one there would refuse to when the milling called for it. But when Greb retreated it wasn't one of those Marathons that Field Marshal Erwin Rommel described as "strategic" after scramming all the way from the gates of Alexandria clear across the African desert to Tunisia, a mere fourteen hundred miles. When Greb retreated it was orderly and for one purpose: So that, having backed up, the momentum on the forward march would catapult him into more devastating action. But since, in a recent novel, someone else has come up with the title that fitted Greb so well, Give Him to the Angels will have to do.

He has been up there with the angels for nearly twenty years now. No matter how many times they may have encased his fists in boxing gloves and sent him to the post against their toughest angels — and there are plenty up there who tangled with him down here—I would vouch for his comportment if—well, there are many ifs, not the least important of which is the referee. He just didn't like referees, especially the ones who called him for such extracurricular activities as sticking his thumb into an opponent's eyes. To him, fighting was so much necessary nonsense anyhow, like getting drunk, so why put a third man in the ring to see that the boys behaved?

Sometimes that third man didn't do so well. He did so badly the night Greb slashed Mickey Walker to pieces in their middleweight championship clash that twice he had to pick himself up off the floor. Not only that, but he was recuperating on the ropes a considerable part of that fifteen rounds of mayhem that still has an older generation gasping and holding on to their seats.

While no one saw the blows or the shoves that twice dropped Eddie Purdy that night nearly a quarter of a century ago, it is significant that in his corner between rounds Greb expressed the thought that Purdy was favouring Walker in the clinches.

"That meddlesome cop," he snorted, "had better keep his hands off me."

Hot water was what he was in most of the time, but the heat agreed with him. He was forever being barred from boxing in one state or another because of roughhouse tactics the very thought of which would chill a Commando's spine.

He was in court for one thing or another, sometimes hailed there by his manager.

At least once a wailing chorus girl waited for him at the altar and the next day she wailed for publication. Greb's rebuttal squared everything as far as he was concerned: "I didn't think splits took me that serious."

When he took off in his car, a rakish speedwagon reputedly given him by a famous Pittsburgh lady, the betting was seventy-five to twenty-five, with Greb on the long end, that he would upset it, injuring everybody but himself. Once, however, he let his backers down. He wound up in Pittsburgh's West Penn Hospital with enough internal injuries, compound fractures and lacerations to kill a mule (animal), but not enough even to slow down the kind of mule he was. While Pittsburgh newspapers were posting death watches and news services were sending out advance obituaries, he was en route to Indianapolis or vicinity to fight rough-and-tumble Chuck Wiggins, who outweighed him a good thirty pounds.

The primrose path was where he did his heavy roadwork. On the eve of a fight his manager knew where to find him—bouncing up and down the stairs in the red-light district, a hussy under each arm and a brace bringing up the rear, while the madame put in a frantic call for fresh stuff. If there is one thing that will ruin a fighter it is clubbiness with a lady before a bout. He knows that if he indulges himself—and it is a temptation that nearly drives him crazy because he can't get from his block-of-granite sparring partners or his roughneck manager the kind of affection rugged youth is fondest of—he will vomit the first time he catches a solid punch around the heart and he will have to swallow it to keep his opponent from getting wise. Greb used to sneak girls into his dressing room, lock the door and give them the works while his opponent waited for him in the ring. Then he would lope out of there, warm and enthusiastic after such pleasurable endeavours, and turn in the most brilliant performance of his career.

As a result of these hi-jinks, all sorts of fables grew up about him after his death. It has been written not once but hundreds of times that he boxed with a glass eye most of his life. Nothing could be more ridiculous. A jarring jolt to the face or a sideswipe across the eye with an open glove would have knocked it out of its socket, to say nothing of what would have happened if a direct hit were scored. Besides, an opponent who wouldn't take note of a glass eye and concentrate his fire on it before the end of the first round would be dopier than Don Quixote jousting at windmills with his lance. Greb was twice a champion. He didn't fight dopes, but this is not to say some of his opponents didn't come under this classification after he had batted them around for eight or ten rounds.

What none of them suspected when he was ranging the fistic horizon, and what only two or three people in the world knew, was that he was blind in his right eye and had less than half sight in his left. He fought at least a hundred major bouts when he was so blind in his "good" eye that, sitting in his corner, he couldn't tell his opponents from their handlers across the ring in their corner. But he didn't quit the ring because of this. He had reached the stage where, in the street, he had difficulty telling a woman from a man ten feet away save for the swish of her skirt or the smell of her perfume.

"Women, he said, "mean more to me than anything else on earth. If I can't see 'em, I can't love 'em, so I'm hanging up my gloves."

It has been written that he fought six times a week and twice on holidays. "The only thing wrong with that statement," he once said, "is that I drop from ten to fifteen pounds in a fight." He thought the sports writers ought to give him enough of a breather to put some flesh on his bones.

The press, not exactly discouraged by the fighters and their managers, paid plenty of attention to boxers who came out of the first world war. It referred to Tunney, who usually entered the ring with a Marine insignia on his dressing gown, as the Fighting Marine. It billed Bob Martin, the A.E.F. heavyweight champion, as Soldier Bob. It went off the deep end for Georges Carpentier when he came here to train for the Dempsey fight twenty-five years ago. With no desire to play down this advantage in one of the most stupendous publicity build-ups ever given a prizefight, Carpentier came into the ring that July afternoon behind a squad of France's famous Fighting Blue Devils, the tricolour dangling from his silk boxing trunks, the band playing the Marseillaise.

It was all very colourful. Sports writers loved to dish it out and the public loved to read it. It paid handsome dividends at the turnstiles. It was smart from every angle, and this is no attempt to criticise it, but—

How many people knew that Harry Greb, who got enough bad press notices to break the heart of a, less rugged individual, enlisted in the Navy soon after America entered the war in 1917, that he mopped up on everybody in the Atlantic Fleet and boxed in inter-allied bouts in London following the armistice? Outside of Pittsburgh, his home town, you could count them on your fingers.

If newspapers outside of Pittsburgh knew about it they kept it secret. There were some mighty odd men on some of the more remote journals back there when Greb was in his prime in the early 20's. A handful of them tried to shake him down with promises of writing beautiful words about him, but when you shook the Greb tree you could expect the falling fruit to knock your brains out. One of these journalistic pimples came up with a sore backside and another lost a mouthful of teeth. Still another waited until Greb died. Then, in his column, he labelled him as "a tightwad who somehow managed to die broke." Greb wasn't a tightwad and he didn't die broke. He made a million dollars in the ring, but spent most of it taking care of brokendown athletes, buying fancy clothes, and having gay parties.

He was a stranger to the reporters who picked on him. They had seen him fight, yes. But they didn't know him personally, had never even interviewed him. If they had they might have handled him the way Harry Keck, Havey Boyle and Chester Smith handled him in Pittsburgh. They gave him hell when he needed it, which was often, but they threw him bouquets too. His explanation for unnecessarily rough tactics got him out of many a tight squeak: "Prizefighting ain't the noblest of the arts, and I ain't its noblest artist."

One reporter in particular viewed him through jaundiced eyes. Covering Greb's fights as he saw them, some of his stories were classics. A fairly typical lead ran like this:

"They tossed pop bottles, clubs, rocks and pigiron at Harry Greb as he left the ring last night. Maybe if Harry had kept his thumb out of his opponent's eyes long enough to let him get his bearings it would have been a different story."

Greb would huff and puff and send word to the reporter that they were through forever, the end of a long and beautiful love. Then he would turn in a nice, clean fight in which he wouldn't have thumbed his opponent more than a dozen times, or nudged him ungently with his knees in the clinches, or stepped on his feet, and the reporter would write that Pittsburgh's Little Lord Fauntleroy had performed creditably indeed. Greb would be delighted and the next day he would hustle around to the reporter's office and tell him he was his sweetheart and demand to know whoever said he wasn't in the first place.

This reporter didn't always pat him with such light-hearted barbs, but he always gave him credit for being on the dead level. When the referee said..."and come out fighting," that's the way Greb came out. No-one on earth could tamper with him. One day a gangster handed him a bale of fifty-dollar bills and told him to drop the decision in his next fight, a couple of days away. It was a fight of no consequence. Greb wouldn't have cared much if he lost it provided he gave his best—and he always gave his best. He threw the money in the thug's face, knocked him down and kicked him all over the street. Only a few feet away, crouched behind a machinegun in a parked car, sat three killer-pals. Greb knew they were there and they knew he knew it. They didn't have the guts to cope with that kind of courage and they got out of there in a hurry, leaving their man gasping for breath and bleeding in the gutter.

Fast as sin and indestructible as rawhide, Greb was seldom knocked down, but when he was he bounced up off the canvas like a jealous stallion, charged with the ferocity of a rattlesnake and clubbed you silly with as hateful a pair of hands as the prize ring has ever seen.

It has been written so often that his name was Berg that a large percentage of sports fans—and many sports writers, too—think it was. He was born Edward Henry Greb, but changed his first name to Harry when he started boxing. An older brother who died was named Harry. Edward Henry, who idolised him, took his name. Greb's father, Pius Greb, now-dead, was of German-American descent, his mother, still living, Irish, which throws down the story that for business reasons he changed his name to Greb simply by spelling Berg backwards.

He never bothered to deny inaccuracies like these so long as they weren't insulting. Consequently, some of the boys went the limit when they hadn't anything else to write about. Shortly before his retirement 1926, a magazine ran an article about him that was wrong in almost every detail except that his home was in Pittsburgh. A friend bumped into him a few days later and wanted to know if he had read it.

"I heard about it," Greb said unconcernedly.

"You didn't read it?" asked the friend in amazement.

"No, but I hear it was a lulu—wrong from start to finish."

"You can make the magazine retract it, and you should."

"Why should I?" Greb grumbled, irritated at being pressured "Some cub probably wrote it and if I denied it it might get him into a jam with his magazine."

"Cub my eye," the friend hung on courageously. "He's a syndicated columnist and he's as well known as you are."

"Just the same," Greb said, simmering down, "he didn't say anything mean about me and maybe it gave the readers a laugh."

He stepped back and looked down his nose like a bad boy about to admit a truth that was going to hurt.

"I'm no angel, bub," he said. "Ha, ha, ha! I done some things myself which wasn't so cosy and I'm not gonna beef about a story I never read and don't intend to read. If he (the author) had a good time writing it, swell; I had lots'a good times myself."

He wasn't lying, either. He had lots'a good times. He had a perfectly marvellous time one night in Grand Rapids, Mr. Harry Greb of Pittsburgh vs. Mr. Chuck Wiggins of Indianapolis. They had had lots'a marvellous times together, but this one was outstanding. It merits the "Mr." before their names. "Mr." lends dignity. This was a dignified evening.

For the younger generation, a little background on Mr. Wiggins: He was a tough cookie. Known as the Hoosier Playboy, he fought all the good heavyweights, tangling twice with Tunney, and he gave them fits. Fighting was what he was fondest of and it didn't matter whether it was in the ring for money or in the street for relaxation. He ran amok in an Indianapolis hotel lobby one night and it took a squad of policemen and several firemen to tame him. "The lobby was a shambles," said an Associated Press story, leaving it to the reader to deduce that Mr. Wiggins wasn't. He got mad at his brother-in-law one day, swatting him on the jaw, and in return stopped a bullet with one of his thick ears, peeling off a sizable hunk of non-edible cauliflower.

Mr. Wiggins' weakness was whisky. Mr. Greb's women. When Mr. Wiggins had finished with the bottle he amused himself and his friends by corralling cops and bumping their noggins together. Of him it was said he could name the town in a given locality in which the cops had the toughest and most tuneful noggins. Of Mr. Greb it was said he could name the town in which the girls' skirts were the swishiest and their manner the most obliging.

So on this evening in Grand Rapids—this outstanding evening Mr. Greb, - his hat pulled down to hide his cocked right eye into which a thousand thumbs had been stuck, sauntered into Mr. Wiggins' hotel room. It was only a few hours before they were to engage in fisticuffs at the local arena, and Mr. Greb said like this: "Hullo Chuck o' pal. You lookin' in the pink. Say kid, there's no use in us killin' each other like we been doin'. Whatcha say we make it a nice clean fight tonight? No rough stuff."

Mr. Wiggins, who looked like a man any sensible bulldozer would choose to skirt, was in a jovial mood and he replied as follows: "Hullo Harry old sock. You're lookin' good yourself. I can properly state, with reference to tonight's engagement, that you have took the words right out'n my mouth.

We made a lot of cabbage fightin' each other and we will make more. We won't pull our punches tonight, but we will make it a nice clean fight like you say. Shake."

It was an agreement between men who respected each other and it was meant to withstand the vicissitudes of time.

Everything was sweet and lovely in the ring, with Mr. Greb complementing Mr. Wiggins on his gentlemanly behaviour at the end of each round and with Mr. Wiggins doing likewise. Comes up Round Four. For some reason unknown to science Mr. Wiggins lunged in a most ungentlemanly and dastardly manner at Mr. Greb, who stuck his foot out and tripped him. Mr. Wiggins fell headlong through the ropes, his head coming to a thudding rest on the ring apron. His large backside did not follow, however, but stuck upright inside the ropes. Mr. Wiggins eased his feet to the floor gently, as in a slow-motion movie, leaving his backside exposed across the middle rope. He didn't remain in this position long enough for nature to grow a pair of hands to protect this seldom-exposed bulge, nor did it occur to the referee to hang a warning light on it, so Mr. Greb leaped in and sprayed it with a dozen resounding wallops. When Mr. Wiggins got his backside in an unexposed position and his head inside the ropes there was a lot of hilarious fun. At the end of six rounds of butting, heeling, biting, kicking and other forms of delightful deliriums, Mr. Wiggins was walking backwards and complaining of bells in his head, and Mr. Greb's faith in humanity had suffered an irreparable blow.

"I will never again trust a man who tells me 'I can properly state that you have took the words right out'n my mouth,' " said Mr. Greb mournfully. "But in all fairness to Chuck, I can properly state that he is the best butter I ever butted against."

Greb was no waster of punches. He aimed them at his opponent, but if they missed and hit the referee — well, what was wrong with the referee? Didn't he have two hands and two feet the same as Greb? Suppose Greb gouged his thumb into an opponent's eyes in the heat of battle, or sank a tooth into his ear, or used his head as a battering ram, or ripped the skin off the face by raking an open glove down over old cuts, or "sneak"-punched on the breakaways, or jumped gingerly on his feet in the clinches? Maybe you wouldn't run across anything like this at Eton. It isn't likely a governess would advise it as rudimentary training for her young charges. But it was the kind of treatment Greb liked to dish out, and when he got it back he didn't yell teacher.

The night he piled up off the floor in Pittsburgh after picking a thumb out of his right eye—a retaliatory thumb to be sure—and knew the sight was gone forever, did he squawk to the referee? On unsteady legs he lowered his head of pain, charged, and handed Kid Norfolk the pasting of his pugilistic life. Back in his dressing room after the fight he swore to secrecy Happy Albacker (a character with whom I shall deal later), then dismissed the tragedy with "That black boy's got a tougher eye than I HAD!"

He came on from there, blind in one eye and with no more than half sight in the other, to win the American light-heavyweight and world's middleweight titles before he died following a minor operation on his nose in an Atlantic City hospital and to inspire such sobriquets as The Iron City Express, The Invincible, The Pittsburgh Windmill, The Inexhaustible, The Wildest Tiger.

He was fistiana's Peck's Bad Boy. Boxing officials threatened to throw him out of the ring at the first suspicion of a foul. Newspapers condemned him. Crowds booed him, not always but frequently, no matter if, as was often the case, he was sixty pounds lighter and six inches shorter than his opponent. Sometimes he fretted on the eve of an important fight, not because he was afraid of his opponent but because boxing commissioners were gunning for him and he didn't want to get the bounce. But he wasn't built to fret long and by ringtime he was relaxed as a cud-chewing cow, the picture of peace and contentment.

"And why not!'" he used to answer when you asked him why he wasn't nervous. "I'll be fighting in a few minutes, won't I?"

That was it. He was a fighting man from the tips of his artistic fingers right down to the gnarled toes of his big feet on which so many retaliatory heels had been ground. Fighting was his profession and he loved it.

It was the same old story when boxing officials stormed into his dressing room, shook their fingers under his nose, called him every vile name in the book and then, winded, shouted: "And we'll throw you out of the ring and bar you from boxing in every state in the union if you heave a single foul punch tonight."

And it was the same old story when his dressing-room door flew open and he shuffled up the aisle to the ring in a nice clean dressing gown, his black hair plastered down, his face freshly scrubbed and his eyes as innocent-looking as a fawn's. This old story went "Boo boo boo boo boo boo!" By the time he had reached the ring the customers had revved it up, leaving out the spaces between the boos, thus:BOOBOOBOOBOOBOO!"

It was no laughing matter and Greb didn't laugh. He slid into his corner as quickly as possible and sat there, his face as sombre as a mortician's. He didn't make himself conspicuous by jumping up and bowing around the ring when he was introduced, but bowed with the timidity of a backward boy unsure of the reaction.

Once the gong rang he was a fox behind leather paws. His lithe body was made of rubber and when he was performing in front of a particularly hostile audience he yanked himself up at the waist and took in foul territory punches that otherwise would surely have landed in fair. Speed was what he had an abundance of and when he turned it on plenty was buzzin', cousin. He ran in on body swings so fast that their timing was destroyed and they often landed in the vicinity of his shoelaces.

The customers couldn't believe it no matter how many times they saw the performance. Here was reputedly the ring's dirtiest fighter, yet here he was being fouled at every turn, never once fouling back, never once looking protestingly at the referee—just a sweet-dumpling who had been wantonly maligned.

Pretty soon the referee was warning Greb's opponents to "Keep 'em up'!" And by this time the customers who had been booing him were yelling "Foul him back, Harry!" Greb usually acknowledged this welcome advice with an owlish smile and from there in, his good character established, you hoped there was among the spectators someone who would notify his opponent's next of kin.

Commander Gene Tunney, retired and only living undefeated world's heavyweight champion, will tell you Greb was the wildest tiger who ever clawed beneath klieg lights. They fought five times. The only defeat in Tunney's career was at Greb's slashing hands in their first bout. It was one of the bloodiest fights in ring history, with Tunney the bleeder.

Chapter II

What's a Floosy For?

Simplicity and directness were Greb's creed. In the ring he depended on speed, withering and relentless. Out of the ring ditto.

At the very height of his pugilistic brilliance—this was before he had ever fought for a title—he phoned me one night and told me to meet him at a gaudy Broadway cabaret that attracted the not-too-discerning guzzling trade during and immediately after the first world war.

"I need you quick," he said. "Pour on the speed."

When he put it that way, you poured on the speed. He would do it for you if the shoe were on the other foot and he wouldn't ask questions. Maybe that's why Hemingway put him up there on that lofty perch with Washington and Lincoln and Schnozzola Durante. Maybe Hemingway knows about the time one of Greb's stablemates, a bantamweight who, having taken a shellacking in Erie, Pa., the night before, stopped off the train in Youngstown, Ohio, the next day and moped into a saloon to try to forget.

The bantamweight was just a kid. He was minding his own business at the end of the bar. An enormous bruiser walked over and squinted at his busted nose. "So you're a pug?" he smirked. Twice the pug's size, he hit him in the mouth, ripping out seven stitches the doctor had sewn on the inside following the Erie bout.

Someone spirited the bruiser away and the bartender came over to the little pug and offered sympathy.

"That guy," he said, "is a sonofabitch. This ain't the first time he has socked decent people at my bar. I got some boys who could take care of him, but his old gent runs this town. I gotta lay off, otherwise I get closed up."

The little pug said it was a hell of a note when a respectable citizen couldn't catch a drink on the fly without being molested. "But," he said, "I can do something about it if you can hold him here a few hours until I get reinforcements."

The bartender promised to detain him. "But," he warned, "you'd better get classy reinforcements because this bird is a mad man when he's drinking. He's a professional football player and tough as hell and knows how to handle himself in the clinches."

"Pal," the little pug said, blood gushing from his mouth, "that's my department. You keep him here and I'll do the rest."

He put through a, long distance call and told his story through numbed lips. In just about two hours the reinforcements trotted into the saloon, shuffled down to the end of the bar where his little stablemate was standing in semi-seclusion, juked down so nobody could see what he was doing and handed him a roll of tape.

"Bandage my hands, kid;" he said. "Let's see your mouth....Hurt the hell out of you, didn't he?"

He threw a quick glance down the bar.

"Is that the bastard down there? Swell.... Okay, kid. Pull the tape tight."

Greb flexed his fingers.

"Good," he said, "good tape job. We'll take care of your mouth soon's we get out of here."

The little pug told him what the bartender had said about the bruiser being tough. Greb gave him one of those so-what's-the-difference looks.

There were a lot of people at the bar now and several cops were standing outside; the bartender had been phoning friends for two hours. Before Greb set out to avenge his little pal he wanted to know how many other men he would have to slough. Not that it mattered, because there was a chair within reach and he knew how to use it if he ran into more trouble than he could handle with his fists, but he was meticulous at odd moments like this and wanted to know what the score was.

"Ah those other guys," the little pug said, "will move away when you move in."

Greb and his stablemate strode down the bar and, as the bartender had promised, everybody moved away from the bruiser. The latter put his hands up, but before he could use them Greb drove left and right to the mouth. The big man went down—he outweighed Greb by seventy pounds—and there was a gap in his mouth where pearly white teeth had been a punch before. He jumped up and tried to hold. Greb thumbed him in the eye, blasted him with both hands under the heart and puke poured out of his mouth. Greb rushed him into the wall, bouncing his left knee off his groin en route, then held him with one hand while he rattled his head against the plaster with short, vicious chops to the chin with the other. Greb stepped back. The big man fell face down in his own puke, his eyes closed, blood oozing out of his twisted, torn and semi-toothless mouth.

"The time," someone yelled, "forty-seven seconds."

The cops came in, smiling, and said it was clever work. Leaving, Greb put his arm around his little stablemate. "Your mother's not here to look after you," he said with a touch of big-brother irritation, "so I gotta do it."

"Mother couldn'ta did better," the youthful pug said.

"Know what?" Greb asked. "This'll cost you two girls. Know any here in Youngstown?"

"Just a minute," the little pug said. He went back to the cops, who were cleaning up the bruiser, holding smelling salts under his nose and saying it was too bad they hadn't been there when he was so brutally set upon, and they gave him half a dozen addresses.

"Holy Toledo," Greb yelled, "we ain't got time to go to all of them places. Our train leaves in forty-five minutes."

"How about my mouth?" the little pug asked.

"Open," Greb said.

The little pug opened his mouth. Greb peered into it. 'It's much better than when I first saw it. We'll take care of it in Pittsburgh. Doc Disque will fix you up. Come on, let's go see the girls." He went to two houses and he had a wonderful time.

On the train back to Pittsburgh, where he was boxing 220-pound Captain Bob Roper (Greb weighed 151 and they were thrown out of the ring for fouling), he wanted to know the following about the Erie bout: (That guy butted you over the eye; did you butt him back?; you know what I told you about butting first. (2) You shouldn'ta went up there without me, you dope? (3) Who refereed? Did he know you was my pal? (4) I suppose you put on the gentleman act and tried to look fancy. Humph!

The little pug tried to answer, but Greb wouldn't let him; there was more important business at hand. "What,?" he asked, "is the name of that new dame we met at Dimling's? Remember, you wrote her name down last week? Hot-lookin' number. I would like to see more of her. Don't think she would give me no trouble." He smiled and indicated that what he meant by "more of her" was when she was naked, stripped for action.

So when Greb phoned some four years later and told me to meet him at that Broadway cabaret in a hurry, I remembered Youngstown and I poured on the speed.

Greb was sitting next to the dance floor. With him, her head buried in her arms on the table, was a girl who obviously had been crying but now was only sniffling. Everybody in the cabaret, which was packed, was glowering at Greb who was returning glower for glower and forcing nearby glowers to break ground. Sinister-looking men and their women were uttering strong words of condemnation—"The lousy bum," "Where's he t'ink he's at?", "He oughta be boined in erl," etc. Greb was sitting on the edge of his chair exactly as he sat on a stool in his corner waiting for the gong to send him into action, but none of his condemners ventured beyond the condemning stage.

I sat down as inconspicuously as possible. Just then a, faraway voice wafted through the churlish atmosphere and came out "Boo, boo, boo, boo" at our table. Other voices picked up the refrain and synchronized it so perfectly that you felt the walls would tumble down if some one didn't get out of step soon. It was so familiar a sound that Greb's mouth parted in a sheepish smile. It took you back to the Arena in Philadelphia. You saw Greb, an outlander from across the mountains in Pittsburgh, hauling his thumb out of the eye of some local pride, an angry crowd rushing the ring and uniformed cops, clubs drawn, yelling "Git back there or I'll split yer heads down the middle!"

I asked Greb why all the furore. He didn't say anything for a good two minutes; he was waiting for someone to start something, but no one did. Then he got up, glowering defiantly and turning his battered features around so he wouldn't miss anyone. He dropped a twenty dollar bill on the table. Shuffling out, indignantly as a wet hen, he snapped: "Pay the check and take this floosy home."

Floosy! Even before I saw her face I knew she was a million-dollar baby. She raised her head and dabbed at her moist eyes with a hand kerchief and I recognized her immediately as Olive Thomas, a much publicized Ziegfeld beauty whose charm had made many friends and influenced even more people. I couldn't describe her better than play reviewer John Chapman described Carole Landis in her Broadway debut of A Lady Says Yes: "...Something of a national monument in human architecture who even in repose looks as though she'd just taken a deep breath."

The booing had stopped with Greb's departure, but shifty eyes were on me from all over the cabaret. These were not the circumstances under which I would have chosen to interrogate this heavenly body, to get at the bottom of all her tears and all those boos for my pal—not with so many narrowed eyes that suggested guns, brass knuckles, stilettos, blackjacks and other instruments of conviction. Besides, it was my first meeting with Miss Thomas. I was still a kid, a heroine worshipper, and here was my idol — a breathtaking beauty who made your heart race. I couldn't think of anything to say until, finally, I remembered she was originally from a Pittsburgh suburb. I didn't know which one, but I thought that if I mentioned some of them she wouldn't think I was such a stranger. It would put us on a commoner ground. She let me name them...Ben Avon...Dormont... Crafton.. Coraopolis... Sewickley.

"You know Pittsburgh, all right," she said, and there was a flicker of a smile around her pretty mouth."The best sports town in America," I said pridefully. "There's Pitt, Carnegie Tech, Duquesne and, not much farther than you can kick a football, West Virginia University." (I didn't mention Greb, but I wanted to.)

It was the punch-line I needed. She gave me a big, sustained smile, practically wilting me, and when I glanced around the cabaret I noticed that the tension was off there, too.

There was a lot of talk around us now. Men were saying Miss Thomas was a slick chick and that she could put her shoes under their bed any time. Girls were gushing at her beauty and her clothes. Of course, there was an occasional sour note from envious men who wondered out loud who is that little egg with that delicious skirt.

This particular cabaret was no place for the sweetheart of Broadway, but Miss Thomas, sweetly if not truthfully, allowed she had been in worse. The waiter brought back the check. While we waited for him to return with the change from Greb's twenty-dollar bill I asked her what had happened.

She reached over and touched my arm confidentially.

"I would rather not tell you here," she said quietly.

The waiter tried to outstay me with the change, but finally gave up, returned and slammed it down on the table. "Cheap skate!" he said with all the meanness that could issue from one sour mouth.

The properly brought-up Miss Thomas was horrified.

"You aren't going to leave that crude domestic a tip, are you?" she asked with charming naivete.

"It will be safer if I do," I said knowingly.

"Perhaps," she said, "this is a rowdier place than I had suspected."

I left a tip. We got out of there fast and walked a couple of blocks down Broadway to the Palais Royale, where Paul Whiteman was becoming famous as the Ring of Jazz. By now Miss Thomas was giggling. The air, and Greb's departure, had done her good.

"If you still want to know what happened in that frightful place," she said, "I'll tell you. But first I want you to know I'm no prude. I don't embarrass easily. I'm a show girl and I've been around. I know all the boudoir answers, the gentle ones and the coarse ones."

"Greb didn't teach you any new ones?" I asked, knowing that he kept abreast of such things.

"Well, not exactly. The circumstances were what confounded me. And it didn't help—"

Paul Whiteman turned the spotlight on her and motioned her to take a bow. She took a bow, just a baby bow, and got a terrific hand.

"And it didn't help," she picked up her story, "to be called a floosy and to have Greb drop that money on the table. It looked as though, via you, it was in settlement for services rendered."

"Don't be silly," I said. "He wouldn't have thought of pitching you less than a thousand. He knows a bargain when he sees it."

The Palais Royal was rapidly filling up. The headwaiter was delightedly telling new arrivals Miss Thomas—she was married to Mary Pickford's brother Jack but they were separated—was sitting over there to the right of the dance floor. Everybody was looking at our table. You could tell they agreed with the considered judgment of the noted cover artist and portrait painter, Harrison Fisher, who had called her "the most beautiful woman in the world."

"If we stay here," she said, "I'll have to whisper. Isn't there a quieter place? I can't give this story its proper nuance if I have to whisper."

We found a place on a side street where she didn't have to whisper. But she sat down and didn't say anything. I had the feeling that, although the barrier had been down only a few minutes before, it wasn't now. I had been flip before. Now I was timid. She seemed to be weighing the advisability of continuing the story. Did she think I looked too juvenile? Did she think I didn't know the answers? How could she think that of Greb's pal? I wanted to reassure her, but I was afraid that if I tried to it would only confirm her suspicion. This was my first experience with a glamour girl—a real, authentic Follies stunner whose pictures I had seen in a hundred Sunday supplements. I never felt so helpless, sitting there beside her, glancing at her, then glancing away, pretending I was thinking about something else. You couldn't sit near Olive Thomas and think about anything else but Olive Thomas. My heart was pounding. I couldn't talk. I began to fidget. Suddenly, she said "Oh!" the way so many professional beauties do when emerging from foreign thoughts. And just as suddenly the barrier was down.

"Now," she said, "I'll tell you about Greb."

He had come to New York the day before with a note of introduction from a mutual Pittsburgh friend. Miss Thomas wasn't working in the Follies, but was visiting friends backstage in the musical hit Irene.

"How he knew I was there," she said, "I'll never know. But he came backstage and handed the note to me. I received him warmly, as I always receive people from home, and I could see that he mistook it for the rush act. His face showed it. It showed that if ever he had doubts as to whether a girl was itching, simply itching, for his presence, he wasn't having them now."

He gave her a fast survey job, stepping back and, like a pug exercising his neck muscles so that when he gets hit around the head his neck won't be broken, gave her the once-over with such concentrated vigour that it all but ripped her clothes off. And what he saw delighted him to the point of remarking that "You've got some swell shape there, Olive. I think I'm gonna like you. Let's bounce out and have a piece of whisky and a talk."

Miss Thomas glanced inferentially at a little man, a typical stage-door Johnny, who was about to collapse under the weight of a bundle of American Beauty roses. Greb's interpretation of all this was that she would gladly accept his invitation if it weren't for this little man.

"Him?" he said as perfunctorily as he would jab a thumb into an opponent's eye. And just as perfunctorily he reached out and pushed the little man down, burying him beneath all those roses.

"There were a lot of people backstage," she said. "I was afraid there would be a riot, so I told Greb to come with me and we left."

"Direct to the cabaret?" I asked, knowing that although he seldom drank anything stronger than ginger ale, he usually squatted at the first saloon he came to so as to get the girls in the proper mood without wasting time. The cabaret was eight blocks away."

"Direct," she said, "and we were recognised the moment we entered. You could hear them saying 'There's Harry Greb the prizefighter and Olive Thomas the Follies girl.'"

Ten minutes after they had taken a table up against the dance floor Greb reached over and put her hand in his. "Mind you," she said unbelievingly, "we had met only ten minutes before and it was our first meeting."

She took a deep breath, revealing a figure under breasts upon whom nature had been lavish.

"I'm crazy about you, Olive," he said in one of those low voices that somehow travels a city block. "How do we stand?"

Miss Thomas, who had suave millionaire playboys at her feet, was evasive. She had to be in those glittering days following World War I, when taxes were negligible and shoeshine boys had country estates at every intersection.

"I admire you as a pugilist," she said.

"Fine, fine," said Greb in the manner of a business executive bestowing commendation upon a helper, "come down to my hotel room and let's——." He named the word and it was heard all over the cabaret, but if I named it here those Boston booksellers and/or the Watch and Ward Society would maybe go on a witch hunt aid ban the story of the man Whitey Bimstein, his colleagues at Stillman's, Broadway Rose and others do not consider underneath the war. "Truthfully," she asked, "what do you think of that?"

I said Greb wasted no punches in the ring and none out of it, that he didn't know how to beat around the bush. He didn't believe in old-fashioned courtships lasting, say, an hour or so. Here he was with a beauty from home. They were both famous, both in good health. Then what was wrong with a little cohabitation?

"Precisely the way he felt," she said, her eyes agleam. "But did he have to yell for everyone to hear? Couldn't he have whispered, or written a note, or made signs? Failing this, he could have said, 'Hey, Olive, how's about pulling up your skirts for a pal?' But there we were in plain view and easy hearing of all those rowdy people, with his voice carrying a block, and he blurts out that awful bathroom word. I didn't know what else to do, so I hid my face in my arms and cried."

It is difficult to identify that Miss Thomas with the one who died so tragically following an overdose of sleeping potion in Paris some months later. Greb, who was all heart, was saddened when he read about it. He said he couldn't reconcile it with the pert, stunning, brilliant beauty of the stageboards.

"Maybe I didn't handle her right," he said sorrowfully, ("but she could have been more co-operative. Where I went to school we were taught to ask for what we wanted, not make signs. Olive knew what——meant. If she didn't want to do it she could have said so. Okay, sister, I would have said, if you don't know what's good for you, go ahead being a dope the rest of your life."

In death he forgave her, but in life never. A short time after their unsuccessful meeting he announced plans for a barnstorming tour of the Pacific coast. Miss Thomas was now back in Hollywood, where, reputedly reconciled with Pickford, she would continue in pictures.

"I'm gonna look up a lot of pals out there," he said, naming Douglas Fairbanks, Thomas Meighan and a slew of others who put their money on his nose every time he climbed through the ropes, "but there's one little dunce I'm not even gonna let on I know. You know who she is. She had her chance to yank her panties and make us both happy, and she didn't do it."

"She has a better shape than any girl in Hollywood," I said.

"I'll admit that," Greb said grudgingly, "but I wasted a whole night (it was all of half an hour !) finding out that all she does with it is throw it around on the stage."

Chapter III

Cobb Was Good, Too

Greb's youthful ambition, which clung to him all of his life, was to be a baseball player. He had been brought up on stories of the Flying Dutchman, otherwise Honus Wagner, the fabulous shortstop and batting ace of the Pittsburgh Pirates, who was in his prime at about the time Greb was beginning to feel his athletic oats. America was more baseball than prizefight conscious then. The headline grabbers in 1910 were Ty Cobb, Tris Speaker, Walter Johnson, Christy Mathewson, Rube Waddell, Napoleon ("Nap") Lajoie, Chief Bender, Home-Run Baker, Mordecai ("Three-Fingered") Brown, etc. And, of course, that never-to-be-forgotten Tinker-to-Evers-to-Chance combination.

Greb wanted to be like these diamond greats. His father, Pius Greb, was telling about this in September, 1944. Old Plus, who was to die six months later, was passing his eighty-third birthday painting one of his houses, which was next door to the Greb home- the home where his fighting son was born. He was jumping around on the roof with the agility of a monkey chasing its tail. His wife, eighty-two, had done a huge washing and hung it out to dry. Her only complaint was that "I have a little rheumatics in my right wrist."

I had gone to their home with Happy Albacker, Greb's confidante, and Harry Keck, the Pittsburgh Sun-Telegraph sports columnist. It was a humid, wretched day and I was about to collapse from (1) the heat and (2) a hangover. But the Grebs, twice my age, were behaving like a couple of healthy, industrious children.

Keck's photographer wanted to snap Pius, but the old gentleman, vigorous in health and stubborn as a mule—a slightly faded carbon copy of his son—consented only with the understanding the photographs would not be published. With some cajoling, after posing for the first shots, he scampered down the ladder that was almost vertical against the roof trough—it made us dizzy watching him—and he talked, in pronounced Germanic accents, about "my boy." (Old Pius was born in Germany and spoke five languages.)

He didn't say he had closed his home to him when his boy returned late one night in 1913 and admitted he had engaged in a professional fight, his first. We knew all about it, though, how, after denouncing prizefighting as a, rowdy business, he opened the door and said, "No boy of mine who engages in it can live under my roof. Get out." His boy got out, never to return except as a visitor, but he held no grudge and he respected his father as does any appreciative son brought up in a well-ordered home.

Old Pius' conversation, which came reluctantly and only through delicate prodding, dealt almost exclusively with his boy's talent as a baseball player. He said he had wanted him to be a stone mason, that stone masonry was safer and more dignified than any field of sports, presenting the convincing argument that, in particular, "it is better to be a live stone mason than a dead prizefighter." But mostly he dwelt on his boy's gift for baseball, emphasizing and re-emphasizing it. From his gestures, reserved though they were, I visioned his boy hitting all over the field, pulling down a, difficult fly here, another there, running in on bunts the pitcher had failed to take and bringing down the grandstands with sensational put-out throws to first. Albacker and Keck shared this vision, too, for they kept glancing querulously at each other as old Pius haltingly unfolded the story we had never heard before.

"Yes," he said uncontroversially, "my boy was very good at baseball. He should have followed baseball."

He had nothing to say about his fistic life, and for a good reason other than his opposition to it: He had never seen him in the ring and no amount of coaxing could convince him that he should, not even after he had won his second championship, the middleweight. It was plain he would not discuss anything he disliked so strongly.

His nearest approach to it was when he told how when his boy was in knee pants he wouldn't fight boys who picked on him. "He ran away," he said. He didn't say he was a, coward, he merely said he ran away. His expression remained the same when he said, "Then one day I saw four bullies, all bigger and older than my boy, grab him and tie him to a wagon wheel. He broke loose, and he ran them down, and he whipped them so thoroughly that I never saw them in our neighbourhood again."

We thought we had old Pius now, that he would go on from there and tell us what he thought when he saw his boy's name splashed in big headlines across the front pages of Pittsburgh newspapers after annihilating Tunney for the 175-pound title and three years later, successfully defending the middleweight title, sent the slashing, hardhitting Mickey Walker, himself a world's champion, to the Missing Persons Bureau for identification. But all he would say about his boy, called by many the greatest fighter, regardless of poundage, who ever lived, was that "My boy was very good at baseball. He should have followed baseball."

En route to downtown Pittsburgh, Albacker and Keck waited for the other to speak. They waited a long time, these men who love to talk and who talk so well. They crossed their legs, then uncrossed them. They shifted in their seats. As if I had been holding out on them, they peered at me the way a speakeasy lookout peers suspiciously through the peephole at a customer. Keck finally broke the spell. "Hap," he said, "say something. Why, for instance, if Greb was as good at baseball as old Pius claims, didn't I know about it? Why, also, didn't he sign up with the Pirates?"

"I can think of no more valid reason," Albacker said, his eyes dancing and a strange expression on his handsome, kindly, strong face, "than that Jim— that was his nickname for Pius' boy Harry-was beyond doubt the worst baseball player on earth. Jim couldn't have caught a baseball if he had been the Pentagon building and you threw one into it. I saw him, when, mind you, he was middleweight champion of the world, play on a kid team one afternoon and the opposing fourteen-year-old pitcher fanned him every time he came to bat. I've seen him try to catch a baseball a thousand times. If it didn't bean him, knocking him for a loop, he missed it by ten feet and fell on his face for his efforts. Jesus, was he awful! I tried to shame him out of making a fool of himself, but he, like old Pius, thought he had the makings of a baseball star and every time he spotted a sand lot team he got into the game if they'd let him."

We were coming into sight of Forbes Field.

"You know," Albacker said, nodding toward the Pirates' ball-yard, "I don't think Jim ever forgave Barney Dreyfus for not putting him on the club."

Was it conceivable that Greb didn't know he was a fizzle as a base ball player? Didn't he know that he hadn't even the qualifications of a bat boy?

"Search me," Albacker said. "But I think it simmers down to this: He knew that no matter how brilliant he glittered in the eyes of the pugilistic world, he was a blackout in the eyes of old Pius. A big league uniform would have changed the story."

Disappointment dripped from Keck's face. Just as kindly as Albacker, and just as staunch a friend of Greb's, he was lost for words. He had gone off the deep end for Greb when he was an unknown preliminary boy. In his column, he had told Pittsburgh Greb was made of the stuff whence champions come. He said Greb was a fighter from hell, a fury fighter and newspapermen who didn't think so would have to eat their words. He was ready to fight Greb's detractors. He took an awful kidding around from contemporaries, but it wasn't long until they had to pull in their horns. Greb came to his rescue. Still a kid, he was, he was knocking the ears of men like Willie Meehan, Big Bill Brennan and Gunboat Smith — all of whom had given Dempsey trouble and one of whom (Meehan) had outscuffled him. Greb was only a heavy welterweight, weighing around 150-152 and all of these men were full-fledged heavyweights. Pretty soon what Keck thought about matters pugilistic carried weight. Tex Rickard, this country's moat famous boxing promoter, never made an important match without consulting him.

"I take my ace photographer out there,'" Keck said. "What a set-up for pictures! There was old Pius skittering around on the roof on his eighty-third birthday with the grace of a cat. We got swell shots - shots that would in a measure tell the story of how Greb came by his amazing endurance. They would tell the world how this medium-sized man (five feet eight inches), who at his best fighting weight was never heavier than a hundred and sixty, could spot good, big men up to seventy pounds and make them wish they had never been born. They would tell the story of why Jack Kearns would never let his rough, fast, hard-hitting tiger (Dempsey) fight Greb except in the training ring."

Keck sniffed repeatedly and jerked his head nervously the way he used to do when his favourite fighter was in there belting the daylights out of some unfortunate opponent. We used to cover those bouts together. He would lean against me in the press section, spraying me as he talked, and wonder out loud why in the hell anyone ever took up fighting as a profession when there were guys like Greb around.

Continuing, as we sweltered in the taxicab, he said: "Weren't those the ingredients for one of the swellest sports-page picture stories of the year? And what happened? Old Pius said 'No, you cannot use them.' Bad enough, you will agree. But why did the old goat give us that baseball nonsense?"

Albacker said it was simple as a b c.

"You saw how he arched his back and looked like a crotchety old cow every time we tried to draw him out on boxing. He's a baseball fan himself, an admirer of the Flying Dutchman. He wanted Jim to be a baseball player. Never mind that he had sired the toughest ring warrior of our time. Old Pius washed his hands of that folderol and quick like a rabbit he made him into a baseball player—a very good baseball player. He knew that no friends of Jim's would challenge him because Jim never did. He gave us the business and we, three wise men who know the answers, had to swallow it. If that isn't one for the books, I'll eat you for dinner at the William Penn tonight."

I told Keck that if I were he I would disregard old Pius' wishes and write the story for all it would stand and use the pictures.

"No," he said, "never. If I did, do you know what would happen? I can see old Pius standing beside a grave in Calvary Cemetery, waving a copy of the Sun-Tely. The earth would belch, and into the air a, six-by-four plot of sod would shoot like an oil-well gusher. Before him would stand his boy, yanking at green boxing trunks with his forearms the way he used to do as he slid out of his corner at old Madison Square Garden. 'What's cookin', Father?' Greb would ask. Old Pius would tell him and the Sun-Tely would be looking for another columnist."

"You're not kiddin'," Albacker said. "See this?" He started to demonstrate, then changed his mind. "No, it's a better story this way."

He had gone to suburban Oakmont, where, at the Razzle-Dazzle Club, Greb had agreed to put on an exhibition for club members. A brawny blacksmith from the neighbourhood had boasted he would temper him as he did horseshoes, then hammer him into shape. Greb didn't

think this was a very sporty attitude for his opponent to take, since, if you accept it in the strict meaning of the word, an exhibition is an affair in which you do not hit for the kill but tap ever so lightly. However, he thought it would be a healthy experiment, he being quite a student of attitudes himself, especially sinister attitudes, so he took Albacker along for the purpose of giving an eye-witness account following the exhibition. As Greb was getting into ring togs, he went into his No. 1 attitude. The blacksmith, taking note of this, excused himself, bolted out of the Razzle-Dazzle Club and was never seen again. "Jim grabbed me," Albacker said, "handing me a pair of boxing trunks, and he told me to get into them. I Said no, that I was drunk, but he said to go ahead anyhow, that we would just clown around for the amusement of the Razzle-Dazzle boys. That's what we were doing, with Jim pushing me off balance occasionally and Spinning me. Everybody was enjoying it. Suddenly, I was possessed of the devil. Don't ask me why, but I cocked my right — you know how I could snake it in there! - and with Jim thinking it was part of the clowning set I crashed it against his jaw, dumping him. He jumped up any imbecile could see he was in the wrong attitude. Before I could convince him that I wasn't responsible for my actions he gave me this." Albacker reached up and took a big bridge out of his mouth.

"Before I made that awful mistake," he said mellowly, "I needed this (bridge) about as much as you'd need ice at the North Pole. Jim said he was awful sorry, but that was after he had cooled off two hours later."

So Keck, as always, obeyed his own dictates and he didn't use those pictures of old Pius.

Chapter IV

Flooded (With Love) in Johnstown

Enter now Mr. Cuddy De Marco, a very classy little man, and also foxy, when the gong rang; He was one of Greb's stablemates. By the time he had reached full maturity, he weighed 130 pounds—if he stuffed himself with bananas, drank a vat of beer and put lead in his shoes. Nevertheless, he worked as a junior lightweight and, as age sneaked up on him, a lightweight and a welterweight. He was fairly well known around the fistic loop, which was a tribute to his skill, because you had to be a superman even to be heard of if you boxed out of Greb's stable.

It was of Mr. De Marco that Greb made a classic remark one hot evening that should be engraved on copper and placed in the cornerstone of our next skyscraper so that if this civilisation is ever destroyed the new one will know that no matter what our faults were, we at least had one great humorist. Greb was standing at the corner of Broadway and Forty-third Street. At this stage of his career you could have accurately guessed his profession if you had never seen a pugilist before. His nose had stopped plenty of leather, and there were other evidences on his features that told a mute story of tough struggles inside the squared circle. Mr. De Marco ambled up-Greb had been on the move and hadn't seen him for some time—and after a racy exchange of pleasantries ambled on. Greb summed up the meeting this way: "Guess who just came by? Cuddy De Marco, and you know the damned fool's got a busted conk and looks just like a prizefighter."

Mr. De Marco made a lot of money in the ring, and he deemed it wise to emulate Greb, so he dropped it all around as he skipped gaily along the Primrose path. Even now, though his chosen trade is far behind him and he is weighted down with family responsibilities, he is rated a skipper-dipper by the lighter element of the Pittsburgh whose rugged sons have ever been a match for the metal spewed up by all those blast furnaces. Don't forget old Fritzie Zivic, allegedly a kindergarten classmate of Methuselah, who is still a hard man to handle, with or without his thumbs in gouging position. And there's Billy Conn. Before these two champions, there were Middleweight Champion Frank Klaus, and Big Frank Moran, and Fritzie's brothers Jack and Pete. Then there's Commando Kelly, who grew up on the wrong side of the tracks but got over on the right side long enough to snuff out a trainload of Hitler's men in the recent European unpleasantness. Pittsburgh does not forget her people.

But I mustn't stray from Mr. De Marco. He was down for an engagement with Tony Ross in Johnstown, Pa., a, couple of weeks before Greb was to leave for New York to start training for the Mickey Walker bout in 1925. He dearly loved to talk like a queer and otherwise ape them by swishing his hips around. If anyone decided to do something about it—such as bopping him on the beezer - Mr. De Marco would try to talk him out of it, but if his dialogue wasn't convincing enough to avert ugliness, why he could take care of that very nicely.

'Listen, darling," he said to his celebrated stablemate, "how's about you running up to Johnstown and seconding me against Tony Ross tomorrow evening, then I'll go to New York with you and help you get ready for Walker." (Greb used to work out in the gymnasium with Mr. De Marco, who moved around fast, thus keeping him sharp.)

"Okay, squirt," Greb said. Greb wasn't a big guy himself, but he looked like a giant alongside the tiny De Marco. They were pals. So, arm-in-arm, they shuffled off to Johnstown. As Greb was taping his chum's hands in the dressing room the promoter rushed in with what he said were unhappy tidings.

"So-o-o-o!" said Mr. De Marco, squinting his eyes and looking bored. "What happens?"

"Tony Ross don't show up."

"Takes a run-out powder?" said Mr. De Marco angrily.

"I don't know for certain what it is he takes," the promoter said, "but whatever it is he ain't here, and they ain't no substitute your size I can t'row in wit' you. Too bad, Cuddy. I lose a lot of greenery and so do you."

Fifteen hundred dollars was the amount of greenery Mr. De Marco stood to lose if he didn't fight someone that night in Johnstown. This was a, dilemma, and by no means a, mild one. The good Lord had been kind to Mr. De Marco in the mental department. He had given him a head to be used as other than a target for vigorous young men to toss punches at. And now was the time to use it.

"Darling,'" he said enthusiastically to his stablemate, "let's you and me put on a exhibition. You're gonna work with Mickey Walker in a couple of weeks. You've been getting a lot of publicity, and now's the time to cash in on it and at the same time save fifteen hundred potatoes for me and make some for yourself too. Whatcha say, sweetheart? The fans will eat it up. You're the Champ."

While Greb was by no means a braggart, still it didn't make him unhappy when a pugilistic smarty like Mr. De Marco addressed him as Champ.

"Smartest idea you ever have," beamed Greb, with an eye on the other end of the purse and no risks involved. "I need to limber up anyway. Cuddy," he said, "I'm beginnin' to believe some of them stories I been hearin' about how brilliant you are. You sure are brilliant."

"I never even went to college," volunteered Mr. De Marco.

"No, but you got a lotta stuff in that little dome of yours," said Greb flatteringly.

The promoter lauded Mr. De Marco for coming up with such a brilliant piece of thinking, but he said he would have to let the customers decide. He said he was pretty sure they would stand for an exhibition, especially with Greb exhibiting, but since they had paid to see an official fight in which the principals would be pegging for keeps, he would have to feel them out on the switch in plans. He went out into the ring, picked up a megaphone, and gave them as colourful a sales talk as has ever been heard by human ears. And it worked. In unison, the customers yelled "'Fetch out that wild tiger ! Give us Greb !'"

Back in the dressing room Greb was having difficulties. Precisely, he was trying to squeeze into a pair of his little stablemate's boxing trunks, having deposited his own paraphernalia in the baggage room at the railroad station. When he finally jammed himself into them- he was out of training and had been stocking up on starches - there was a roll of fat around his middle as big as the Belgian bulge.

"Don't move me around too fast," he told Mr. De Marco, "because I'll bust out of these as sure as hell and I'll be pinched for showing my can."

"It won't be the first time you've ever been pinched, and for less reason," Mr. De Marco said cheerfully. "Besides, don't worry. I'm gonna, imitate the slow train through Arkansas tonight."

Greb laughed heartily at this rejoinder and remarked that Mr. De Marco sure was slaying him with rapid thinking.

They loped out into the ring, The referee instructed them about this being an exhibition. "You men know," he said, "this is only for fun. I guess I don't have to tell you that, because you're pals."

The gong rang. These stalwart fellow townsmen touched gloves in the traditional good sportsmanship gesture, smiling sweetly. As Greb squared off leisurely, Mr. De Marco came in with a fast banging right to the chin. Greb hit the deck. For a couple of seconds there sat the world's middleweight champion, and hovering over him like a cross little elf stood his stablemate who was only two weight divisions bigger than the smallest fighting man in the professional ring. Mr. De Marco weighed 126 pounds minus all that stuff he had to poke down his gullet in order to get up to the junior lightweight class.

Greb scrambled up.

"You little wop bastard," he said bumptiously, "whatsa idea o' socking me like that?"

He threw his long arms around Mr. De Marco and clinched. He was almost a foot taller and correspondingly heavier than his little stablemate and he was smothering him. Mr. De Marco yelled to the referee to protect him. Freed, he backed up, talking, and this is what he said:

"You big lug, you've been pasting my ears off in the gym for years and having a lot of fun and there wasn't nobody to stop you. But there are plenty of people out there, and I'm gonna shellack you, and if you slug me they'll mob you."

Greb recognised the logic behind this statement.

Mr. De Marco heaved everything he had at Greb and Greb didn't dare hit him back with noticeable venom. The fans wouldn't stand for a big guy socking a pee-wee like Mr. De Marco. Finally, after Mr. De Marco had turned a deaf ear to please to be nice, Greb grabbed him. "Now I'm gonna fix your wagon, you wop bastard," he advised.

He rakes an open glove down over Mr. De Marco's battered features, ripping off generous hunks of skin, and repeated this procedure as often as he could get inside his arms in the comparative seclusion of a clinch, smiling ingratiatingly for the edification of the fans. He was killing Mr. De Marco, who did the best he could in these painful embraces. He bit, kicked, butted like a billygoat.

At the conclusion of this exhibition (Webster's definition of an exhibition is ". ..a work of art, or of feats of skill"), the Messrs. Greb and De Marco left the ring from opposite corners. En rout to the dressing room, with Greb in hot pursuit and about to bust out of his boxing trunks, Mr. De Marco picked up a dozen policemen and implored them to form a cordon around him. He said his life wouldn't be worth a plugged nickel, and neither would theirs, if they didn't handle the situation with the utmost tact. Mr. De Marco said it would be better for all concerned, but for Mr. De Marco in particular, if they called out the state militia.

The cops handled the situation admirably. At Mr. De Marco's behest they used no strong language and made no threats. Otherwise, they would have been sorry because Greb, like his old pal Chuck Wiggins, was a handy man at bumping noggins together. Even with the cops around him, Mr. De Marco waited a, comfortable distance for Mr. Greb to cool off. Greb gave no indications that he ever would until it suddenly occurred to him that the train for New York was coming around the mountains. It also occurred to him that Mr. De Marco had the only available berth, which he had picked up in Pittsburgh, and the ticket for it in his pocket. Greb had an appointment the next morning with Humbert Fugazy, who was promoting the Greb-Walker fight. There was no other train that would put him in New York in time to keep the appointment, and he was a man who kept appointments, especially when they were connected with a big-money bout or a date with a doll.

So he switched from the belligerent to the charm department. But it wasn't that simple to convince Mr. De Marco that all was forgiven. Mr. De Marco continued to huddle close to his protectors. As Greb would approach, turning on all the charm at his command, Mr. De Marco, quaking, would cower behind the cops and say, "No, no, no, chum. I don't like the look in your eyes."

As the train neared, however, the Greb look got pleasant enough for Mr. De Marco to take a chance. They piled onto it, shared the lower berth together and came on to New York, where Mr. De Marco helped put his stablemate in shape for the Walker fight. Mr. De Marco took no unnecessary chances in his work-outs with him at Manhasset. He always waited until a big Crowd had gathered, lest Greb, who had an elephant's memory, got to thinking about Johnstown and became technical about having forgotten and forgiven. Mr. De Marco didn't do Walker any favours, either. He put Greb into such fine shape that Mickey barely escaped with his scalp.

Chapter V

The Bell Saved the Referee

For an active pugilist, Greb was an old man now: thirty-one. He had long since lost the sight of his right eye and his left was beginning to dim under the same kind of rigorous treatment to which he had subjected opponents. His once marvellous physique had begun to creak under the strain of twelve years of ring warfare and more than two hundred and fifty fights up and down and around the fistic horizon ... Omaha ... Tulsa ... New Orleans ... St. Paul... Milwaukee ... Newark ... Los Angeles ...Philadelphia . . . Oakland . . . Baltimore. . . Wheeling. . . Boston . . . Bridgeport . . . Cumberland . . . Steubenville . . . Youngstown . . . Chicago ... Kalamazoo ... Grand Rapids ... Punxsutawney ... Wilkes-Barre ... Buffalo ... Indianapolis ... London ... on the high seas when he was in the navy, etc. As if this were not handicap enough, he had to get down from 174 to the middleweight title poundage of 160. It was excess weight caused by age. It was hard to shed and he had given himself a bare two weeks to do it. He didn't believe in heavy training, arguing that boxers who pursued it often left their fights in the gymnasium.

"If I'm gonna leave mine any place," he chuckled, "it'll be on a Beauty Rest with some skirt. I'm open to suggestions if anybody can name a pleasanter way."

This was the way Greb had always talked and this was the way he talked on the eve of what he knew would be the hardest fight of his brilliant, slashing, plunging career.

Mickey Walker was young, a terrific hitter, disrespectful, rough, wise, and he was welterweight (147 pounds) champion of the world. But he couldn't make the weight any more end retain his best fighting edge. He was stepping up into the next division, the middleweight, and this would be his first start against big-time opposition. Unlike Greb, he had no weight-making bugaboo to contend with as long as he didn't get up above 160 and he had no intention of doing this. He had nothing to worry about. If he lost, his public would say it had taken a bigger man to beat him. His title wasn't on the line, either; no matter what happened he would still be the welterweight champion. If he won he would take the bows for dethroning one of the greatest champions of all time and on his head would rest the crowns of two world's titles.

He didn't love Greb and Greb didn't love him. Neither had said anything about it for publication, realizing if he did it would smack of insincerity. The fans would say it was the old come-on calculated to break down the turnstiles in the expectation of witnessing a grudge fight.

This kind of talk would have been superfluous anyway. The fans were going to be treated to the unusual spectacle of seeing two world's champions pitted against each other. These weren't run-of-the-mill champions, such as the New York State or the National Boxing Association version, but the acknowledged and undisputed kings of their class.

Greb trained harder for this than for any fight in his career. To assist him he had, among others, Mr. Cuddy De Marco and Mr. Patsy Scanlon, two very capable little men. Mr. Scanlon is now an almost forgotten gladiator except in his home town of Pittsburgh, but he deserves a nod and he's going to get one if this ancient L. C. Smith can stand up under the additional verbiage.

He was one of the best left hookers around. He was cunning. When he was in there with a toughie he sometimes resorted to the timeworn ring psychology of nettling him with uncomplimentary fast talk. To wit, only this one—well, you'll see.

Mr. Scanlon was boxing Dick Loadman one lovely evening 'neath a beautiful Pittsburgh moon. Loadman was a sharp, dangerous puncher. It was shortly after the first world war. Married, he hadn't gone into the service.

"You hid behind your wife's skirts," said Mr. Scanlon scornfully as the referee broke up a clinch.

Loadman didn't say anything, but a couple of rounds later he measured Mr.; Scanlon, nailed him with a deft, vicious right on the chin and glued him to the canvas for the nine-count. When Mr. Scanlon staggered up there were still cobwebs in his brain.

"Are you still interested in why I didn't go into the army?" Loadman asked sharply.

Mr. Scanlon said no, he had no further interest.

"In case you develop one," Loadman said, slamming both hands to the mouth and bringing forth a flow of blood, "I was sleeping with your sister."

The re-telling of this charming episode in the hectic life of Mr. Scanlon pleased Greb no end. For that reason, plus the added one that Mr. Scanlon gave him good work-outs in the training ring, he frequently included him in his entourage.

Originally Greb had planned to train at Madame Sitky Bey's at Summit, New Jersey. Then he remembered that the sweet old madame had all but raised Walker, and besides Summit was too far from Broadway. So, stocking his larder with an ample supply of girls he had picked up in Pittsburgh and way stations en route to New York, he pitched camp at Manhasset, Long Island, and settled down to the simple life of (1) being the sultan in his harem and (2) trying to shed weight. At nights he breezed into New York, corralled other girls, moved them around rapidly on the dance floors at the Silver Slipper, Jimmy Kelly's, etc., and usually got back to camp in time for breakfast in the morning. This had always been his routine. It didn't meet with the unqualified approval of his manager, but this disturbed Greb about as much, say, as socking an opponent or getting socked after the bell had ended the round. His optimistic faith in the integrity of managers - and he had three different ones at odd times - seldom got beyond the stage of permitting them to carry his luggage.

Yet for all his nocturnal activities he found time to run a few miles on the road and work eight or ten rounds daily, always using good, fast, fresh sparring partners. In contrast to most "name" fighters, he permitted them to extend him if they could. If they extended him on a day when he had got up on the wrong side of bed he extended them back. Mostly, he trained with smaller men. They were faster than bigger men. Greb was a speed merchant and he trained for speed. More than once these little men ganged up on him after he had ruffled their tender feathers unnecessarily and there was a riot in the ring. But he forgave them as soon as the storm was over. Not only that, but when a stablemate got beaten in actual combat Greb would sometimes go gunning for his opponent and if he caught him he would slap his ears off.

Previous to the Walker match Greb's training usually consisted of punching the small bag a couple of minutes for rhythm, skipping rope, playing a sizzling game of handball and maybe boxing two or three rounds. This occupied twenty minutes of his time, which he considered a sheer waste. (Tunney and Dempsey spent more time than this exercising their neck muscles.) Then he would yank out his huge address book and thumb through it for the hottest telephone number in whatever city he was going to box in. By the time reporters had begun to foregather to put critical eyes on him he was the middleweight champion who wasn't there and he was taking the kind of (horizontal) exercise that was no trial to any man. All that ninety-eight per cent of the Fourth Estaters knew about him were the unlovely things they saw him doing to his opponent a few nights later in Chicago, Boston, Memphis or Montreal.

This was particularly true of New York. He didn't pitch camp in the country as other champions do while surrounding themselves with press agents, photographers, and movie starlets anxious to get their pictures in the papers. Greb worked out at Philadelphia Jack O'Brien's gymnasium deep in the heart of the Great Whiteway where there were girlie shows whose performers would listen to reason.

But now, in 1925, he was exposed to the pure Long Island air and it was suffocating him. In other days he fought two-three times a week. He was always in shape, always ready to enter the ring against anyone at a moment's notice without as much as limbering up in the gymnasium. Now, up to June 5, he had worked in exactly fourteen fights and the Walker fight, on July 2, would be his next. There aren't fighters around today (and he was only one of them) who could stand up under a schedule half as strenuous. The inactivity (for Greb) had a bad effect. He was flabby and, for him, slow. He had to do something about it so Manhasset was the answer.

Having lost practically none of his excess weight at the end of week of what for him was loathsome labour, he decided on a different course. He quit eating and he drank only enough water to keep from famishing of thirst. He got rid of the weight.

He knew Walker was going to give him a hell of a fight, but he had no doubt who would win. Just before he climbed into the ring Mr. Tom Bodkin, a, Pittsburgh boxing promoter and referee when Greb was coming up and now a Broadway theatrical man, asked him how he thought he would do against Walker.

"Are you getting balmy?" Greb shot. "What the hell do you how will I do against Walker?"

This wasn't the way he talked to men he loved as much as he Mr. Bodkin. But he was amazed that anyone, and particularly Bodkin, could entertain the slightest doubt as to his chances of victory.

Gene Tunney dropped around to see Greb the morning before the fight. He was appalled at what he saw. Greb was gaunt-eyed and so weak from starving off weight, plus the deleterious effect of keeping happiness in his harem, that he was trembling. He had a slight temperature.

These men had fought five times and they were hard fights; Tunney lost his 175-pound title in the first one and, though the decision was unpopular, regained it in the next one. They were sixty-five of the most miserable rounds of Tunney's pugilistic life and he would be the first to admit it. But they weren't going to fight each other anymore and now they were friends.

No matter how Tunney felt about Mickey Walker, he couldn't help wishing luck to his old antagonist. Men who have battered each other as these two had don't often become the fastest of friends. They don't lie awake nights praying for disaster to overtake the other, but there is almost always something that rankles. But it was different in their case; they had made a lot of money together.

Tunney was too smart to tell Greb how sick he looked. Instead, he whipped out a bottle of champagne, a rare jewel in those awful prohibition days.

"Drink this, Harry," he said. "It will relax you."

Greb drank it.

Then he went up to Central Park and ran twice around the reservoir to make sure that when he stepped on the scales an hour later at the New York State Athletic Commission offices he would be within or under the middleweight title poundage.

After weighing in he went to Billy Lahiff's, now Duffy's Tavern, Inc., and ate his first decent meal in ten days. It gave him a lift, but he was awfully tired and he still had a temperature.

He went to his hotel and tried to sleep, but couldn't. Mr. Happy Albacker, a quart of hootch under each arm, came in.

"Put that giggle water down," Greb said, "and gimme a, rubdown." Mr. Albacker put his hands on Greb.

"You're hot," he said.

"Sure," Greb said, "sure I'm hot. If you light a stove, it gets hot, don't it?"

"You got a fever?"

"Sure, and I feel lousy, but I'll be all right. Rub me down, Hap."

Mr. Albacker was something of a cross for Greb to bear, but they were inseparable. He went to work on Greb's arms, legs and shoulders and it worked. Greb fell asleep. When he waked half an hour later he was somewhat' rested.

At seven-thirty he left for the Polo Grounds and was in his dressing room before the opening preliminary was called into the ring.

Jimmy Slattery was glad to see him. Later to become light-heavy-weight champion, he was waiting to go on against Dave Shade. Greb had boxed Slattery in Buffalo a few months earlier. Slattery was just a kid, but he had been performing sensationally. Before the bout, Greb had said to him, "You're a nice-looking kid, Jimmy. You've got a great future in this racket if you keep your chin down and your hands up. Don't pull any show-off business tonight and I'll make you look good in front of your hometown admirers. A deal?" (Greb was middleweight champion, but his title was not at stake.)

He had no intentions of horsing around in the ring. What he meant was that if Slattery gave him a good fight, but didn't show off, Greb wouldn't turn on too much heat. Certainly, he wouldn't mess him up as he did other opponents. Slattery was handsome and Greb meant to let him stay that way.

"I won't show off, Champ," Slattery said respectfully.

He didn't show off and Greb, though beating him, let him look good in defeat. They had lunch following the bout and Slattery said he would dearly love to show in New York. The Greb-Walker match was on the fire.

"Okay, Jimmy," Greb said. "I'll see that you get on the card with me and Walker."

He had kept his promise and now here they were - Greb the wise old warrior, Slattery the young and promising one—sharing the same dressing room.

"Any instructions, Champ?" Slattery asked when he got the call to leave for the ring."

"You don't need any," Greb said. "Only remember this: You're making your first appearance in the greatest city on earth. But the rules are the same here as in Buffalo. You can hit as hard here as any place else. Don't let that big crowd scare you. Keep your eyes on Shade. He's smaller than you are and he's tricky. Smaller men always gave me trouble, but I learned how to whip them; I used my weight and height to their disadvantage in the clinches. That's the way you had better fight Shade. Wade into him. Bull him. Keep him off balance and let him have it in the clinches. Now go out there and slap him around."

Fifteen minutes later Slattery, knocked out in the third, was sobbing on Greb's shoulders in the dressing room. Greb was patting him on the back and telling him to cut it out, that it was no disgrace to be knocked out, that it was all in the game. Hadn't Greb been flattened in an early fight? And hadn't he come on to win two titles?

Slattery just sat there and cried.

Greb was like a mother with her first child. He didn't know what to do, hut he was doing the best he could when Humbert Fugazy, promoter of the fight, rushed in. White with rage, Fugazy said:

("Wills refuses to go on unless he is given main-bout billing." (Harry Wills, who had capitalised for years on his inability to get a bout with Dempsey, was boxing Charley Weinert in the semifinal.)

It was a ludicrous situation. Here was Wills, a good fighter but by no means great, demanding, at the expense of two of the greatest champions in ring history, to be spotlighted.

While Slattery sat there and sobbed, Greb jumped up and raced down to Wills' dressing room. (Wills, 6 feet 3, weighing 220, Greb 5 feet 8 weighing 158.)

"You big tramp," he yelled, "I'll fight you right here in your dressing room and the winner will get the main bout."

Fugazy grabbed Greb. While he was hanging onto him, the boxing commission ruled that Wills, having been billed to work in the semifinal, would have to go on in it. Wills glanced furtively around the room, glad of the excuse to get out of there before Greb broke loose, and he left in a hurry. He knocked Weinert out in the second. Then he leaned his brown body over the ropes, this tall, lean Negro whom Runyon had tagged the Brown Panther of New Orleans'.

"Ah done it wid my lef'," he told a reporter. "Sho' did. Dat ol' lef' was workin' good tonight!"

The main bout was coming up.

Walker was the first to enter the ring. He was smiling confidently and he got a tremendous ovation. The Toy Bulldog, they called him, and he looked it.

Greb came in two or three minutes later. He was pale, his face drawn, and he still carried a temperature. His handlers crowded about him, talking fast and frantically. Everybody connected with him was worried sick. He drew some boos, but not many. That was the way it was with Dempsey; in the twilight of his greatness the fans forgave him for his foul tactics and they didn't boo him so lustily.

Tunney had told Greb that morning, "It's your title that will be on the line tonight, Harry, so make Walker enter the ring ahead of you."

If Tunney was at ringside, as he undoubtedly was, he must have been pleased that his advice hadn't fallen on deaf ears. And he must have been pleased that he wasn't in there against Greb, even a tired, sick and old Greb.

The silvery-voiced Joe Humphreys, premier fight announcer of the day, waved for silence and it took him several minutes to get it. Then he gave the principals the benefit of his booming, flowery tongue:

"Ladies and gentlemen, for the world's middleweight championship, fifteen rounds to a decision. In this corner, the challenger, the welterweight champion of the world, the Toy Bulldog, a Champion of Champions, the sensational pugilist from across the river in Elizabeth, New Jersey—Mickey Walker. The weight: One hundred and fiftytuh."

The cheering was deafening and it lasted so long that Humphreys had to plead with the fans to desist until he could introduce Greb. After several false starts, semi-quiet was restored.

"Ladies and gentlemen—"

The Pittsburgh contingent, which had come in on Greb Specials, showed the New Yorkers that their boy wasn't alone in the big city, It cut loose with enough volume to burst your eardrums. "Puh-leese !" Humphrey begged. "Puh-leese ! Puh-leese!"

There were scattered fist fights among the spectators and the cope were busy breaking them up. Those Pittsburghers were backing their boy not only with money, but also with punches. Maybe the more conservative element called him a trifler back home, but he was their baby when he crawled through the ropes and they had what was needed to prove he was. They were bank presidents, coalmine and steel-mill executives, shoeshine boys, bellhops, society matrons and debutantes, waiters, valets, whores and madames, racketeers and flotsam. Maybe they hadn't even a nodding acquaintance in the street at home, but they were pals when they swung onto those Greb Specials and followed Greb to the scene of battle.

Having showed up Wallter's admirers, Greb's people quieted down. Humphreys took a deep breath. Calling Greb the world's middleweight champion, the Invincible, the Iron City Express, the Pittsburgh Windmill and the Inexhaustible, he announced his weight as one hundred and fifty-eight.

Eddie Purdy, the referee, motioned the men to the centre of the ring, instructed them, and told them to come out fighting at the bell. If ever there were two men who didn't need this admonition it was the two up there under those strong lights with him. Both were champions, both the final word in skill and courage.

The ten-second warning bell sounded and out of the ring tumbled the handlers. There is no place so lonely as when your seconds leave you during that ten-second wait between the warning and opening bell. You're up there with a man who is hostile and who aims to hammer you into submission. The referee is nobody's friend. There are thousands of people all around you, and many of them are your people, but you are lonely as you wait for the bell that will send you into battle. You may be killed. You hope your sins have been forgiven. You think of everything. Then the bell rings, and you move out there, and you are still lonely as you feel out your foe. You settle down a little. Then you start to sweat and you are all right. The warmth returns to, your feet, you are punching smoothly and now you are as comfortable as when you were a little boy sitting on your mother's lap. All you want to do is murder that bum in front of you. It is a lot of fun, and it is remunerative fun.

Greb and Walker stood in their corners sweating out those long, awful seconds. To those who had seen him in his earlier fights, Greb looked like a hollow shell; to those who hadn't, he looked okay. To everybody, Walker looked wonderful.

Greb had expected to take a dreadful beating in the early rounds. He knew he hadn't the stamina to fight off Walker's rushes, but he hoped to come from behind after Walker had spent himself trying to knock him out. He knew better than anyone what woeful condition he was in, but he had a heart that was disputive of his tired, aging and overworked body. That heart had always said no when his legs had said this is the end, pal.

Clang went the bell and out of their corners tore two of the greatest champions who ever shuffled shoes in resin dust. For five rounds that July night in 1925 Greb, old, slow and sick, took one of the most frightful beatings any man has ever had to take. He was fighting back, but his attempts were feeble, and Walker was strong and contemptuous. As he went to his corner at the end of the fifth, his body a mass of red welts and bruises, there were shouts of "Stop it!"

His handlers worked over him, sneaking him a slug of brandy, rubbing his aching legs, massaging his limp arms. He didn't look like a champion now, but you knew about his heart and knowing about it you didn't count him out. You winced as you contemplated what Walker would do to him in the next round, the sixth. How in the hell could he stand up under another round of the pounding he had just taken? You knew he wouldn't quit, not this pug. He didn't know how to quit. You had seen him when he was in trouble before, grave trouble. You had seen him pile up off the floor that time in Pittsburgh when Kid Norfolk had dropped him after blinding him in his right eye. You had seen him in all those hard Tunney fights, a good small man against a good bigger man. And before that you had seen him against the clever, hard-hitting Tommy Gibbons, and Greek Knockout Brown, who could tear your head off with a punch. But that was a young Greb. That Greb was no more. In his place was an old Greb who had gone to the well once too often.

The bell rang for the sixth and what you saw you couldn't believe. Comparatively fresh, Greb jumped out of his corner, moved into Walker and tied him up. Walker stepped back, then came in with a two-handed barrage aimed at Greb's middle. It didn't land. He tried again and missed. He missed again and again. Then Greb ran in on him, spun him and stepped back and hit him while he spun. He didn't hit him once but twice, three times, four times. Jesus, did he clout him! You settled back in your press seat. You were seeing a miracle. The Pittsburgh Windmill was sweeping now, sweeping everything before it. Greb had come back from the depths of despair. In a clinch he glanced down into the press section and that glance said, "Hah! I'm gonna knock this egg down there into your typewriter and he'll be scrambled when he lands. How'm I doin', kid?

As if he had been in low gear to negotiate a rough stretch in the road, he switched suddenly to high and he dared anything to pass him on that roped-in highway pitched beneath klieg lights. He outthought and outfought Walker, as he had said he would. He dazzled him with his speed. The works were what he was giving him and they were the vinegar works. Walker was bleeding, an ear was torn, an eye puffed. With Walker floundering awkwardly, Greb was putting a sour eye on Referee Purdy, the kind of eye you wouldn't want to meet even in broad daylight at Forty-second Street and Fifth Avenue. He thought Purdy was favouring Walker in the clinches. He didn't like referees anyhow, and here was a meddlesome one, an officious man who had better watch his step. He said something to Purdy, but you couldn't hear what it was. You could guess, though, and your guess was, "Lay off, bub. Lay Off me in the clinches."

The seventh round was a repetition of the sixth. As it started, one of Greb's seconds sneaked around to the ringside seat where Mr. Happy Albacker was sitting. He whispered something to Mr. Albacker and Mr. Albacker looked hard to get Greb's eye. He got it. Greb smiled, pushed Walker away and made an odd gesture with his hands. Then with renewed vigour he belaboured Mickey. He kept giving that unpretty eye to Purdy, who was as busy as ever in the clinches. There was another clinch. With six legs locked in combat, you couldn't see who was doing what to whom. Then you saw Purdy, blocked by Greb's right leg, go down. Walker jumped over him and Greb skirted him, chasing Walker. The bell ended the seventh as Purdy got up and limped over and held onto the ropes.

"The bell saved the referee!", yelled Mr. Albacker, a very factual man.

For an instant it looked as if the fight would have to be held up until another referee could be sent in. But Purdy stuck it out. He was limping noticeably as the eighth opened. Greb took advantage of this. He bullied Walker all over the ring, stabbing him with punishing uppercuts and cracking him in the mouth with two tireless, heavy hands. When Purdy came close, Greb pulled Walker away. And when Walker clinched Greb gave him plenty of stuff that is not in the lexicon of any of the fighters around today. When Purdy, limping, tried to reach the fighters Greb waltzed Walker away. Greb was having a wonderful time, Walker wasn't.

Purdy, his knee improved, became active in the ninth and tenth rounds and Greb was giving him the eye. At the end of the tenth Humbert Fugazy hustled over to Greb's corner and cautioned him against any untoward action.

"Lay off Purdy," said Mr. Fugazy, "or he'll throw you out of the ring."

"If he don't lay off me," Greb snorted,' I'll stuff him down Walker's throat."

Purdy didn't lay off in the eleventh. There was a clinch and when all those legs separated he was in the position to which, in this fight, he had become accustomed. Specifically, he was down again. The score up to now was: Knockdowns—two, with Purdy the knockdown. "The Iron City Express is steaming tonight," said a reporter sitting next to me. "They say he doesn't like referees."

Walker had a good eleventh, not so good twelfth, just a fair thirteenth. Purdy was doing the best he could, but he seemed gunshy when he went in and tried to break up the clinches. Greb wasn't doing much, just coasting down the mountain and enjoying the scenery. Walker had a good fourteenth, twice staggering Greb.

Greb opened the fifteenth with a burst of speed that befuddled Walker, who was either crying or laughing, you couldn't be sure which. He was talking to Greb. (After the fight we were told it had been announced on the radio that he asked Greb not to knock him out. Greb said, "That's right. He asked me not to knock him out." Later, he said, "No, he didn't ask me not to knock him out.")

Greb bullied Walker all over the ring in that final round, but Walker, like Greb, was a champion, too. He didn't know how to quit. They were doing everything to each other, and none of it was nice. As the bell ended one of the roughest fights in ring history, Walker was a badly used-up fighter. His mouth was torn and gushing blood. An ear was ripped, and an eye puffed the size of a goose egg. Greb was tired, but there wasn't a mark on his impish face.

Joe Humphreys raised Greb's gloved right hand.

"The winner and still champion!" he bawled, and you should have heard those Pittsburghers break out.

Greb trotted over to Walker's corner where Mickey's seconds were patching up the damage.

"You're a good boy, Mickey," he said, patting him on the back. "You gimme one hell of a fight, the hardest I ever had. You didn't lose your title, and you didn't win mine, so everything's jake, eh kid? But you shouldn't'ta been so rough on the referee!"

Like a frog with a hot coal under its tail, Mr. Albacker leaped over the two rows of seats in front of him and landed in the press section. He proffered a drink from a flask just two gallons smaller than Boulder Dam.

"What," I asked, "was the significance behind all those signs passing between you and Greb in the seventh?"

"Ha, ha, he!", and also "Ho, ho, ho!", Mr. Albacker beamed. "You see Greb's second come over and whisper to me?"

Anyone with half an eye couldn't have missed it.

"Greb sent him over to ask me if that doll with the grapefruit knockers — notice how Greb, when he got my eye, moved his heads down over his stuck-out chest to indicate what he meant? -would be waiting for him at the Silver Slipper after the fight."

I said that I figured that whatever intelligence Greb's second was imparting to Mr. Albacker must have been of world-shaking importance, but with Greb in the toughest fight of his life and only one round after he had taken the upper hand, I couldn't imagine what he was up to when he made those gestures.

"You know now, Mr. Albacker said, "and you know it was of world-shaking importance. If that dame with the large bosom ain't waiting for him at the Slipper he'll beat my brains out."

Mr. Albacker took a big swig from his flask.

("Here, kid," he said, handing over the flask. "Have another horn. Will see you at the Slipper. Will give you a good story about Greb pulling a drunk act the night before the fight, but it ain't for publication."

Mr. Albacker hotfooted it back to his pal's dressing room. Fortunately for him, the dame in question was Waiting when he and Greb arrived at the Silver Slipper. When Harry Keck and I looked in on them a few hours later everybody, including the dame, was having a dandy time. Mr. A. called me aside and informed me that Greb hadn't exaggerated in his reference to the girl's large chest.

"And what's more," he said, "my pal's going to chin himself on them tonight."

No one who saw the Greb-Walker fight twenty years ago will ever forget it. For savagery it rivalled that knockdown-drag-out encounter between Dempsey and Luis Angel Firpo, the Argentinian called by Runyon the Wild Bull of the Pampas.

James Dawson, the New York Times boxing expert, said it was a sizzler. He said Walker had displayed such courage and stamina as had seldom been seen in any ring. "But," he added, "Greb was Greb last night."

Greb wasn't Greb that night, but he was enough of a facsimile thereof to whip Walker, and that was one hell of a facsimile.

Twenty years later Humbert Fugazy remembered a coincidence following the weigh-ins at the boxing commission offices in the Flatiron Building the morning before the fight. Walker had gone to a Catholic church in Greenwich Village. After praying he had dropped in at Fugazy's nearby offices.

"Put your bankroll on me, Humbert," he said. ('I'm going to knock that Pittsburgh Dutchman's head off tonight."

An hour or so later Greb had gone to the same church, not knowing Walker had preceded him, and prayed. Then he went to Fugazy's offices.

"Put your lettuce on me, kid," he said. "When I get through with Walker tonight he'll be an Irish stew, all cut to pieces and cooked."

A thousand stories have been told about the incidents leading up to, including, and following that clash of champions. Billy Duffy, part owner of what once was Billy Lahiff's but now is Duffy's Tavern, Inc., said Greb came into Lahiff's with two girls an hour after the fight and took his favourite table at the right as you enter. Walker came in a few minutes later, looking for his manager, Jack Kearns, who had been barred from the Polo Grounds by the New

York State Athletic Commission. Pleasantly Walker said, "Hello, Harry. You were lucky tonight. If it had been a twenty-rounder instead of fifteen I would have knocked you out."

Greb, according to Duffy, said, "Go On, Mickey. I can whip you any day in the week. Sit down and have a snort."

Mickey sat down and they sipped an ale. Then they left, arguing about the fight, with Greb's girls. Drawing up in front of the Silver Slipper, Greb said, "What I did to you at the Polo Grounds tonight I can do right here in the street."

He started to take his coat off. He got it halfway off.

"Walker hit him on the chin with a short, terrific left hook," Duffy said. "He went down, his head hitting the running board of a cab. He jumped up and they fought there in the street like two crazy men. A cop named Pat Separated them. They went into the Silver Slipper and took

separate tables. Then they bought each other a drink, made up and retired, the best of friends, to a hotel in the West 70's and continued their spree."

Mr. Happy Albacker said no, a thousand times no. Greb never went to Lahiff's after the fight. He went to the Slipper direct from the Polo Grounds. As he was getting out of a cab in front of the night club, Walker got out of one right behind him. Mr. Albacker quotes Walker as having told Greb that Greb was lucky to win at the Polo Grounds, and Greb as having said he could do in the street what he had done in the ring.

"They squared off" Mr. Albacker said, "but someone stepped between them. No blows were struck. They went into the Slipper, took separate tables ant that was the end of it."

Mr. Albacker reasoned, and plausibly, that Walker wouldn't have dared start a street fight with Greb, the master roughhouser of them all. "What's more," he said, "Tom Dolan, who had been in his corner, was with him. I don't need to tell you Tom is the toughest street fighter in Pittsburgh. Tom loved Greb, adored him. If Walker had come within his reach Tom would have wrung his neck—and he could wring any body's neck in a street fight."

Mr. Apples Myers, who used to promote fights in North Braddock, a Pittsburgh suburb, said the street fight is "fiction that somebody made up out of his mind."

Harry Keck, ye olde sports scribe, thinks likewise. "Fighting with out pay," he said, "is against union rules and Greb was a union fighter."

Mr. Jack White, who functioned for a time as Greb's secretary and is now promoting fights for Fritzie Zivic during Fritzie's incumbency in the army, said fiddlesticks, that there was no street fight.

"After what Greb did to Walker in the ring, what do you think he would have done to him in the street where there was no referee to yank Greb Off? Knowing how fast Greb was on the draw, can you imagine him attempting to take his coat off when trouble was brewing. That puts the squelch on Duffy's story."

Another who nixed the street fight was Mr. Tom Bodkin, a close friend of Greb's and, as you will see in a later passage, a man of consequence.

"Greb left the Polo Grounds with Slattery, who had never stopped crying, and bounced around to the speakeasies looking for Dave Shade. If he had found him he would have punched him in the nose for knocking out Slattery."

Still, the story of the street fight persists. Humbert Fugazy said that although he didn't see it he knows from authoritative sources that it is not, as Mr. Apples Myers said, fiction dreamed up by some fertile mentality. And Quentin Reynolds, a man of integrity, wrote a Collier's article about it some twelve years after it supposedly had taken place.

I shall quote from it as soon as I've brought it up to date. Walker is now an artist. At a fairly recent exhibition of his works, an admirer, complimenting him on a painting of the Shrewsbury river, remarked that he was impressed with its texture.

"It has depth," he said.

"Sure it has," Mickey agreed. "The Shrewsbury is a deep river."

Aside from this omission, Reynolds' article is complete. Titled Between Bites, it tells how customers at Walker's bar in the shadow of Madison Square Garden put the bite, or weep, on him not only for money but for drinks as well. Finally, Reynolds got around to asking him if his fight with Greb hadn't been his hardest fight.

The mike is yours, Mr. Reynolds.

"Sure," Mickey nodded, "the second fight with Greb. I think I won that one."

Well, I had never heard of any second fight that Greb and Walker had engaged in and I remembered too that in the record book under the heading Mickey (Edward) Walker there is just one mention of Greb. The line reads "Lost—1925, Greb, 15," and means that Greb beat Walker in a fifteen-round bout to a decision in 1925. But then Walker explained. The first fight ...

Greb was middleweight champion then, and Walker held the welter title. Before the fight Greb was a 7 to 5 favourite hut something happened the night before to scare the gamblers. The something was this: At 2 A.M. Murray Lewin, the fight writer, was Standing in front of Lindy's restaurant on Broadway with a group of the biggest gamblers in the country, most of whom were wagering heavily On Greb. There were Arnold Rothstein and Sam Boston and his brother Meyer, and there were Mike Best and Frankie Marlowe.

A cab drew up in front of Lindy's and out stumbled Greb. Greb waved a drunken greeting to the gamblers and then collapsed. There were two girls with him and they helped him back into the cab. The gamblers looked at each other, white-faced. "That's what we're betting on, hey?" Rothstein said. Then they rushed to phones. They phoned all over the country, betting everything they had on Walker, whom they knew to be in perfect condition. They didn't figure Greb had a chance. You couldn't drink all night and then go into the ring with Walker twenty-four hours later without getting murdered.

The next night at the Polo Grounds Greb, debonair, clear-eyed, climbed through the ropes. The gamblers were laying three to one against him-and he had bet his end of the purse on himself.

"How do you feel?" a sports writer asked, looking up at him as he sat in his corner.

"How did those gamblers like that act I put on for them last night?" Greb laughed.

Oh, but Greb was a cutie. He knew all the angles. The fight was fairly even until the seventh, when Referee Ed Purdy sprained his ankle. This was great for Greb's style of fighting. He kept bullying Walker away from Purdy and he did everything to Mike but kick him in the head. The referee, white with agony, couldn't get close enough to separate them and Greb in close was a murderer. But Mickey was all right too at the Pier Eight style of milling and he was putting up a great fight until the fourteenth.

THEY'D RATHER FIGHT THAN EAT

They'd been slashing and powdering each other plenty, for Greb too was a fighting man who loved to fight. Halfway through the fourteenth Greb bullied Walker to the ropes and he threw a hard right hand. The blow missed Mickey's chin but Greb always was a one for waving a careless thumb. The thumb dropped savagely into Mickey's right eye.

Walker snarled, "You Dutch rat," and then Greb measured him with a right hook. Because of the blood and the water which filled his right eye Walker din't see the punch coming. It landed squarely and knocked Walker out. It knocked him out and his legs were rubbery things that buckled and acted crazily and in his head there was a roaring that grew louder and louder, but Mickey stayed on his feet. He finished the round somehow and then Teddy Hayes threw water on him, held ammonia under his nose, put ice on his spine and with a few seconds left Mickey came to. He had to go through three more torturous minutes. He stayed all right because he had a heart that was strong and that was contemptuous of the weakness in his legs. But they gave the decision to Greb and then Walker went to his dressing room. He got under a cold shower and he stood there for a while and soon the cobwebs cleared away and he remembered something very important.

Doc Kearns, his manager, had been suspended by the N. Y. Athletic Commission and had been barred from entering the Polo Grounds. So he sat at a table in Billy Lahiff's Tavern waiting anxious for Mickey to return. Before the fight Mickey had made a date with a girl and he had told her to meet him in the Tavern. He'd told her to sit with Kearns until he arrived.

Walker hurried dressing. Sure, Doc Kearns was his best friend but it would be just like Doc to try to grab his girl. More than once he'd grabbed girls from Kearns. So Walker hurried and then he went over to the Tavern and as he went in he saw Greb sitting there near the door. He had to pass Greb's table to get to Kearns, whom he saw far in the back with the girl Mike had the date with. Billy Lahiff—bless his memory —stood there and he was a bit nervous. He knew Mike and he knew Greb and he knew that they'd both rather fight than eat.

Walker looked at Greb and Greb looked back at Walker and then Greb got up and smiled. "Sit down and have a drink, Mike," he said, sticking out his hand.

Walker grinned through his swollen lips and he said: "Sure, Harry. I'd love one. I been working all night and need a drink."

"You don't need one more than I do," Greb laughed "Toughest night I ever spent in my life."

So he sat down and had a drink and they talked about everything but the fight. They talked about this movie or that and they talked about the stock market and about how much longer Babe Ruth could last.

Jack Spooner, who has been a waiter at the Tavern for so long that he belongs there like a table or a checkroom, brought two more and Greb and Walker, who an hour before had been doing everything to each other but murder, sipped their ale companionably.

Then Greb said, "Mike, I hear Billy Duffy has quite a place in that Silver Slipper. What do you say we give it a play?"

"That's for me," Walker said, and then they left arm in arm. They got into a cab and went around to the Silver Slipper and then they got out of the cab. Walker suddenly turned to Greb and said, pleasantly enough, "I just want you to know, you Dutch rat, that you wouldn't have licked me tonight if you hadn't stuck your thumb in my eye in the fourteenth."

Greb growled, "Why, you Irish lug, I could lick you the best day you ever saw. Right now I'll lick you."

HE THINKS HE WON

Walker said to me at that point in the story, "Harry made one mistake." Then Walker chuckled, "He started to take off his coat. I waited until he had it half way off and then let him have it. That punch would've knocked anyone out except Greb. It was a good punch and it dropped him and slammed his head up against a cab that was parked there, but he got up roaring. Then we went."

They went, all right. People came out of the Silver Slipper to watch. Cabs stopped and delighted hack drivers watched the continuation of a fight which men had paid fifteen dollars to see a short time before. Every thing went and these two were masters of the forbidden punches. Happily, joyously, they gouged and backhanded and elbowed and punched and then a burly cop roared up end laid heavy hands on them. It was a cop named Pat Casey.

"He was a real right guy, that Pat Casey," Walker says now. "He knew us both and he grabbed us and threw me in one cab and Harry in another and told the drivers to take us to our separate hotels."

Walker got back to his hotel still burned up. So he ordered some ale to cool off. He sat there and as he sipped a glass of ale a sudden thought hit him that almost made him choke. What about Kearns? Where was Doc? He was out somewhere with his—Mickey's—girl.

Walker grabbed the phone and started calling the night clubs. He called every place in town and finally he called the Silver Slipper. Bill Duffy- then and now Walker's best friend—answered the phone.

"Doc isn't here, Mike," Duffy chuckled. "But there's a pal of yours here who wants to say hello."

Walker listened and then he heard, "I can lick any Irishman who ever lived. You yellow rat, why don't you come up here now and I'll lick you again."

Walker was speechless for a moment. "Greb," he screamed into the phone, "you come up here to the hotel and I'll flatten you in two minutes."

For five minutes they hurled invectives at each other. Then the door of Mickey's room opened and Doc Kearns walked in. He caught on immediately. Then he grabbed the phone.

"Listen, Greb. We'll fight you anywhere, anytime, but not in a hotel room or a night club. We'll fight you anywhere, anytime, for fifty grand." Then Kearns hung up.

"Where's my girl" Walker stormed.

"She got tired of waiting for you,'" Doc told him coolly. "Besides she wouldn't be seen with a common street fighter—a barroom fighter like you."

"Why, I'll. . ."

Kearns looked at him coldly. "You'll get to bed before I go to work on you. I'll give you more than Greb did tonight. Hit that hay, sucker, I got some ice coming up."

Walker beamed, "Fine, we'll have another drink."

"The ice," Kearns said, "is for your eye. I forgot to tell you your eye is closed."

Well, that's the story of the second Greb-Walker fight, the fight that Walker thinks he won.

True or false, a street fight between those two men is not out of line with their character.

Chapter VI

Tom Bodkin, Entrepreneur

Financial and social Pittsburgh oldsters knew him - the Mellons, Carnegies, Fricks, Thaws, Olivers. And the Broadway Runyon writes about knows him. He was promoting and refereeing fights when he was in short pants. By the time he got into long ones he was an entrepreneur to reckon with.

If Tom Bodkin had been just another referee and not the student of pugilism that he is, Harry Greb's career might have ended when he was still in the preliminaries and there wouldn't have been anyone, in Whitey Bimstein's estimate, to whom the war was secondary. But before detailing this and his other connections with Greb, I am constrained to report on Bodkin's association with another celebrated Pittsburgh boxer—big, blond Frank Moran, sometimes called the Pitt Collegian. A left tackle on the football team, he left college when it was brought into the open that he was a professional fighter. Like Cuddy DeMarco, he used his head as other than a target for the flailing fists of strong young men whose consuming thought was to destroy. Otherwise, would he have been physical trainer to and personal friend of Theodore Roosevelt?

It was after Moran had fought and lost a twenty-rounder to Jack Johnson in Paris. It was three or four years after he had boxed a no-decision ten-rounder with Jess Willard, who meantime had knocked out Johnson for the heavyweight title in Havana.

Moran had been luxuriating in New York. Broke, supposedly through as a fistic luminary, and on the cuff for six hundred dollars at his hotel, he left town in a hurry one night.

"Much to the annoyance of the cashier and without officially saying good-by," said Bodkin, a practitioner of the subtler way of describing a dark situation.

Arriving in Pittsburgh, he urged Bodkin to take over his management. Bodkin did, got him a match with Denver Jack Geyer, and Moran won.

It put him back into what sports writers like to refer to as the firmament. A millionaire Cumberland sportsman offered to show him against any opponent he cared to name, the fight to be held in Cumberland. Manager Bodkin accepted. The man with whom he had to arrange details was a printer, who was getting out the posters. Bodkin hadn't decided what fighter he was going to pit him against, and he had to decide immediately, so he told the printer to make the posters: "Frank Moran of Pittsburgh vs. Jack McFarland of Philadelphia."

The only heavyweight named Jack McFarland that Bodkin knew of boxed out of Pittsburgh. A very good fighter, too, and life had been unkind to him. But he was dead.

"I couldn't use him," said Bodkin sadly, realizing that what a fighter needs most on the comeback trail is a dead opponent.

In Philadelphia, Al Lippe had a stable of broken-down pugs leafing around and eating him into the poorhouse. Bodkin phoned him.

"Can you send me down a big guy to box Moran in Cumberland Monday night?"

"Why not?" Lippe asked in the manner of a long-headed business man taking care of a customer in need of a scarce product. "I gotta big bird six-foot-three inch which's eatin' me into bankruptcy. How much's in it for me?"

"Two hundred."

Lippe said that would be satisfactory.

"Tell him," Bodkin said, "to be here Saturday so I can walk him around and let the citizens look at him."

"All right."

That seemed to conclude the conversation, but before either had hung up Bodkin said, "Oh, yes, Al. His name will be Jack McFarland. I've billed him under that name, so tell him to register accordingly at the hotel."

"Okay, Tommy." Then as a sort of afterthought Lippe said, "What round do you want him to be knocked out in?"

"The second, Al, and I'm refereeing."

In a deal like this the manager has nothing to worry about because the referee is the final arbiter. It sends him to bed in the peaceful knowledge that if, as often happens, his fighter decides ad libbing is smarter than following script, there are ways of reconverting him. An effective one is for the referee to deftly hold his forearms in the clinches. It is restraining influence, like a hobble on a horse, and it eliminates for the opposition a lot of blood, sweat, toil and tears.

Saturday came, but Jack McFarland didn't. Sunday came, but not Jack McFarland. Bodkin met the Monday evening train. Nothing got off it resembling a six-foot-three-inch brokendown fighter. It was the last train into Cumberland and this was fight night.

Bodkin was in one hell of a fix. He had sold three thousand dollars' worth Of tickets and there was no Jack McFarland to throw into the ring with Moran. He was standing in the hotel lobby contemplating how best to present the heartbreaking news to his tiger when, to the delight of his Irish heart, he detected two objects stealthily descending the back stairs.

They were, no doubt about it, a six-foot-three-inch brokendown fighter, and with him a little brokendown fighter.

Bodkin ran over and grabbed the big one.

"Al Lippe sent you?"

"Yeah," said the big man whose shoulders were wider than the Prairie States and whose body was lean.

"Jesus! Why in hell didn't you come Saturday? I've been going nuts waiting for you."

"I and me little pal come Saturday like Al tole you we would."

"Where have you been?"

"Right here in de hotel, but we stayed in our room. We was eatin' and havin' a good time."

"Eating on me?"

"We wasn't eatin' on nobody else. Al only give us railroad money; he didn't give us no eatin' money."

Bodkin said he had been watching the hotel register since Saturday, that he had just looked at it and there was no Jack McFarland thereon.

"Me name's not Jack McFarland," said the big brokendown fighter. "Me name's See-Saw Kelly."

"You're boxing under the name of Jack McFarland tonight," Bodkin said, pointing to a fight poster.

"Nuttin' doin'," said the big man firmly. "Me, I'm See-Saw Kelly. By de way, is dis bum I'm fightin' the gink which box Johnson and Willard?"

"Yes, and you're taking the count in the second."

"See-Saw Kelly ain' takin' no count for nobody."

The little brokendown fighter took Bodkin aside.

"Don't pay no attention to him. He's just blowin' off steam. I'm in charge of his corner and he'll do what I say. He'll splash in the second."

"Whatever me little pal tole you," See-Saw Kelly said sharply, "don' pay no attention to. I ain' takin' no dive (exiting where indicated on the blueprint) for nobody. 'At big tramp Moran, I'll ice him."

None of this information had been relayed to Moran, who knew nothing about Bodkin's arrangement with Al Lippe.

Bodkin was worried stiff when, four hours later, he went over to Moran's corner and purposefully asked him how he felt.

"In the pink," Moran said cheerfully. "Incidentally, is Mister McFarland going to be a vigorous young man tonight? Will Charles Francis (as he referred to himself in lighter moments) have to go to work on him fast?"

"I don't think so," Bodkin lied, "but don't fool around with him. He's got bats in the belfry, and he's big and hungry and he thinks you're a bum."

"Kerchoo!" sneezed Moran, indicating that was precisely what he was going to do in See-Saw Kelly's battered face.

Bodkin introduced the principals. He introduced See-Saw Kelly as "the sensational Jack McFarland" of Philadelphia and the See-Saw, surprisingly acknowledging it, jumped up and bowed around the ring.

The bell rang. Jack McFarland looked like a champion as he met Moran in the centre of the ring. Moran pulled back his famous right hand—the right hand called the Mary Ann that had brought him up from the obscurity of an unknown football player at Pitt and dropped him into the lap of international fame—the right hand that had intrigued Teddy Roosevelt and supposedly blinded him in one eye during a training session.

That right hand did not land on Jack McFarland, or See-Saw Kelly. Moran yanked it back to the floor and he slung it repeatedly at the big man in front of him. It did not land. If it had, See-Saw Kelly would have been see-sawing in slumberland.

Bodkin followed McFarland to his corner at the end of the round. "You're going out in the second."

"Not for dis tramp."

The little broken-down fighter grabbed Bodkin and, whispering, told him not to worry.

"He's just blowin' off steam like I told you before. He'll do what I tell him, and I already tell him to hit the deck in the second."

Jack McFarland didn't look as though he was going to hit anything but Frank Moran as the second opened. Moran pulled back that right and he heaved it. It missed. He clinched. Bodkin, via his large feet, dropped two hundred pounds of solid heft onto Jack McFarland's toes. McFarland stumbled.

Now was the time to throw that looping right. Moran threw it, and it found its mark, and See-Saw Kelly's face was in the resin dust. Manager-Referee Bodkin counted out the impudent See-Saw, who slept so prettily, so deadly.

As Moran was leaning over the ropes and shaking hands with admirers, See-Saw Kelly jumped up, hit him in the back of the head and staggered him. The fight started all over again. But Bodkin had counted out See-Saw Kelly. The fans had seen it. He stepped between them and stopped it.

See-Saw Kelly had meant to obey orders all along, but he was a cut-up. Bodkin knew this the moment he jumped up and resumed the fight. It was an old trick. It fooled the gullible then and it fools them now. It even fooled Moran, called by Tunney "the most fearless boxer I ever knew...."

Bodkin toured the country with Moran, dissolving their amalgamation following a divided newspaper decision with Fred Fulton in Newark, N. J.

"I never tampered with any more of Frank's opponents," he said twenty-five years later, "and I never told him about my Cumberland strategy. I was afraid to."

There is this story that has gone the rounds for years. One school of thought say it is a lie, the other says it is not. Isn't the same true of Jonah and the Whale?

Frank Moran's star had begun to fade as Harry Greb's began to shine. It occurred to Moran one day that a bout between them in Pittsburgh would be anything but unprofitable to all interested parties. Greb was at least fifty pounds lighter and correspondingly shorter, but he had been rendering even bigger men anemic, so Moran put the proposition up to him. Greb thought it had possibilities.

A sports writer I have never been able to catch up with is supposed to have got word the match was in the offing and he went to Moran's hotel room in the William Penn for confirmation. Moran had been asleep and he came to the door in shorts. Sleepily switching on the lights, he invited him in. And what do you suppose the news-hawk beheld on a twin bed sleeping as sweetly and innocently as a lamb? It wasn't anyone but the scourge of the ring-the Iron City Express.

The reporter, a man of perspicacity, advised against the match on the grounds that if word seeped out about what he had just stumbled onto it might arouse suspicion. He said he understood the fight was going to be ballyhooed as a grudge fight and if it turned out to be anything less the fans might get the wrong impression.

Moran and Greb agreed he had something there. They were so completely agreed, in fact, that they smackdam dismissed as ill-advised the contemplated grudge fight, tumbled into their twin beds and went back to sleep.

However contradictory of Greb's honesty as a fighter this may seem, it must be understood that circumstances alter situations. He was a friend and admirer of Moran's. And Moran, according to the story, had been reduced (through high living) to his last harem. For a friend, greb would do anything. He wouldn't throw a fight—and neither would Moran—but he would engage in one for a needy cause. If the tearful condition of a man reduced to his last harem does not come under this classification, what does?

Greb was knocked out by Joe Chip in an early professional start in Pittsburgh. He was still on his feet, but he was desperately hurt and Tom Bodkin, who promoted and refereed the fight, stopped it. Instead of offering (as most fighters would) the lame excuse that he would have turned the tables if he had been permitted to continue, Greb was grateful. When his head had cleared he told Bodkin,' "One more hard punch might'a ruined me. I won't forget. Tanx, pal." The scene switches to New York nine gears later. Bodkin, who had transferred his talents to Broadway as a producer's manager, was in the same financial rut Moran had been in before they teamed up. Greb had just whipped Tommy Gibbons in old Madison Square Garden and had been matched with Tunney. Burlesque was dying. It needed a shot in the arm. Bodkin went to Maurice Cain, manager of a burlesque wheel. Unfolding a stack of newspapers that had headlined the Gibbons fight, he told him that Greb, appearing as an added attraction, was the man who would lift his shows out of the red.

"He's the new sensation," said Bodkin with convincing enthusiasm.

"He'll win Tunney's title (and he did) three months from now. Then he'll murder Johnny Wilson (and he did) for the world's middleweight championship. Next, he'll run roughshod over Dempsey for the heavyweight crown. (They never fought officially, but unofficially they did—in the training ring—and Dempsey did so badly that when Promoter Charley Murray tried to match them, Jack Kearns, Dempsey's manager, said, "No, thanks. We want no traffic with that Seven-year Itch.")

"How much do you want for Greb?" asked Cain excitedly.

"Thousand a week."

"And how much for you, Tommy?"

"Hundred-fifty."

"Sold. You open at the Gayety in Pittsburgh next week."

Happily, Bodkin went home and fell asleep. Waking in the middle of the night, he wondered why he had slept so fitfully. Then he remembered; he had forgotten to let Greb in on the deal. He hustled down to his hotel, waited until he returned at six in the morning (with two women) and told him what he had done.

"How much is Cain paying you?" Greb asked.

"Hundred-fifty."

"Okay, Tommy. I'll give you an extra hundred a week out of my thousand."

Bodkin had withheld one bit of information; he had arranged a parade in Pittsburgh in celebration of Greb's smashing defeat over the highly-touted Gibbons, a little business calculated to stampede the customers into the Gayety when Greb opened there. Greb didn't care for this sort of display. Knowing this, Bodkin realised there was only one way to get along with him and that was to tell him the score. Whether he liked it or disliked it, he would work with you—assuming, of course, you were his pal; if you weren't, he would spit in your eye if you got in his way.

Bodkin told him about the parade.

"I don't like it," Greb said, "but since you've arranged it I'll go through with it."

Greb looked the two girls over.

"Here," he said, pushing the homeliest one toward Bodkin. "One's enough for me if I'm gonna brood over that damned parade the rest of the night.)'

Bodkin pushed her back.

"Keep her, Harry; keep both of them and make the brooding good."

Three days later Greb paraded in Pittsburgh and that night, with police reserves holding the crowd back, he opened at the Gayety. He had partially memorised a monologue Bodkin had written for him. It went like this:

"It was right here in Pittsburgh that I got my first start in the ring by defeating..."

The rest of it was flowery, laudatory (to Pittsburgh) and long.

After a week in Pittsburgh the show jumped to Detroit. Greb's monologue remained unchanged only it was localised—"It was right here in Detroit..."

He played a week in each of ten cities—cities in which he had fought (and loved) dozens of times. The tour ended in Montreal after a week in Toronto.

By the time he reached Montreal he was slightly mixed up, to wit:

"It was right here in Toronto," he started his monologue "that I got my first start..."

The rough burlesque audience interrupted him with a series of boos. He turned to Bodkin, who was behind the curtain.

"What are they booin' me for, Tommy? I didn't stick my thumb in nobody's eye. I'm breakin' clean in the clinches. What are they booin' me for?"

"This isn't Toronto, you dope, this is Montreal," said Bodkin.

Greb turned to the audience.

"Ha, ha, ha! I made a mistake. I'll start it all over again. It was right here in Montreal that I got my first start in the ring by defeating Soldier Jones...."

"He ad libbed so beautifully," Bodkin said, "that the audience thought it was a wonderful gag."

Even when Greb was doing a favour for a pal, it was not always out of altruism. Churning around in the back of his alert noggin there was often a motive, as in the case of making the burlesque tour.

On a previous trip to Montreal he had entered into a transaction involving six hundred dollars and a diamond stud. The man on the other end of the deal called himself Cohen, the Diamond King.

Back in Pittsburgh some days later Greb had boasted to Cuddy DeMarco, with whom he shared an apartment on Negley Avenue, that he had got a bargain in Montreal such as was unobtainable elsewhere on earth.

"Boo-ti-ful, ain't it Cud?" he asked.

"Plenty of sparkle," admitted Mr. DeMarco, "but I don't think it's worth six hundred clams."

"No?" Greb looked very annoyed.

"Positively no," said Mr. DeMarco, an authority on jewellery, fancy clothes, beak-busting and almost anything you can name.

Under the scrutiny of a Pittsburgh jeweller, the precious stone did not measure up to Cohen, the Diamond King's touting. Said he, "I don't know for sure what this is, Mr. Greb, but I'm pretty sure it is not a diamond."

Mr. DeMarco snickered.

Greb gave him the quick, fierce look of a mad bull as Mr. DeMarco stepped lightly toward the door. Momentarily ignoring his little stablemate, Greb asked the jeweller what he would guess the stone was if not a diamond.

"Off hand," said the expert, putting down his examining glass, "I would say it is a hunk of polished sheep manure."

Mr. DeMarco, who always knew when to run, lit out of there.

Greb made a mental note of the jeweller's diagnosis and he averred he would refer to it the next time he went to Montreal.

"As he moved from city to city with the burlesque show," said Bodkin, "he would look up the mileage to Montreal and he would indicate with ominous gestures exactly the kind of reception that was in store for Cohen the Diamond King."

Now Greb was there and he hadn't once mentioned the diamond merchant. A new girl had joined the show in Toronto. Could this have changed his channel of thought?

"Nothing else but," said Bodkin. "Doused with perfume, his hair slicked back and wearing the blue dressing gown an admirer had given him, he was pacing the floor in our Hotel Mount Royal suite. I asked him why he was so nervous and he said, 'I'm waiting for the new skirt.' "

The phone rang.

"Answer it, Tommy," he said as he rushed into the bathroom to apply the finishing touches to his coiffure, "and tell her to come right up."

Bodkin carried out instructions.

"In a moment the bell to our suite rang," he said. "Greb rushed to the door and yanked it open. There stood Cohen, the Diamond Ring." Bodkin had had a hand in this trickery.

"The disappointment was so great," he said, "that Greb went limp and lost his voice. All he did was motion to Cohen, the Diamond King, to go away. He sat down on the bed and was about to cry. Then the new girl arrived, restoring his faith in humanity. I left and everything was lovely."

Chapter VII

Thunder Over Pittsburgh

Pittsburgh takes its fighters for granted. It took Greb for granted and he didn't like it. He was vain and expected more of a show of appreciation. Then came his fight with Tommy Gibbons. He had been eating green apples, hotdogs and ice cream, a diet Mayo's would scarcely recommend within an hour of such rigorous activity, and he came down with a debilitating case of diarrhoea. Add to this the possibility of getting biffed around the body by a biffer like Tommy Gibbons, and you have an idea of how ungorgeous he felt. He shouldn't have gone through with the fight, but he did and he lost. It was his first loss in two years and he had been fighting as often as three times a week. Only one of the then seven Pittsburgh newspapers, which was by no means the best in town, gave him the decision.

Greb bellowed loudly when he read one account, written by a pal, of how he had lost. He stayed mad at him for more than a year. But he knew he had lost. When the bell ended the fight, he leaned over the ropes, sick, tired and furious, and to those within hearing he said, "Come back to my dressing room and I'll refund every cent you lost on me if you can prove you bet on me."

There is no record that anyone took advantage of his offer, but from that day and until he hung up his gloves in retirement seven years later his work was given the appreciation it deserved. Pittsburgh fans lauded him and they took their little piggy banks to the gambling mart every time he went to the barrier.

The defeat by Gibbons cut deeply into his pride. He could have excused it by explaining about his diarrhoea and no one would have doubted him. But for all his whimsicalities, he wouldn't make excuses, even legitimate excuses, for public consumption. He would lay back his ears and kick defiantly when a decision went against him in a fight he thought he had won-and he thought he won all of them—yet he refused to discredit his opponent by claiming broken hands, illness, wounds from Cupid's arrow or any of the other tiresome routines that are the bleat of so many fighters.

The fans didn't know about those green apples, hotdogs and ice cream, and he wouldn't tell them, but he had to live with his conscience and life was uncomfortable. Too much money had been lost on him and he felt it was his fault. He couldn't face his friends, so he slank off to Conneaut Lake, a Pennsylvania mountain resort, and refused to leave. No amount of coaxing would budge him. Week after week he squatted up there, swimming in the lake and sulking.

On the telephone, he told an inquiring reporter he wouldn't come down until he was guaranteed a return match with Gibbons. Informed that this was not immediately possible, since Gibbons had gone to Ireland to visit ancestors and God only knew when he would return Greb said, "Okay. I'll just set up here till he comes back."

That was the way it stood and Conneaut Lake was where he remained, adamant as a balky mule, refusing to talk turkey to anyone until they produced Gibbons' signature to a contract calling for a return match.

Greb had spoken.

His manager, Red Mason, was going loco passing up lucrative bouts. It was a fate worse than a belly ache for this shrewd man whose livelihood depended on the mainstay of his stable. For him, the sun was behind deep, dark and seemingly impenetrable clouds. Then came word that Gibbons was on the high seas en route to New York.

A committee of Pittsburghers, tears in their eyes, met the boat and sobbed out the story of Greb's indignant hibernation on the Pennsylvania mountain top.

"Please," they pleaded, handing Gibbons a contract, "come over and fight our stubborn boy."

"It'll be a pleasure," Gibbons said. "I can whip that Pittsburgh Dutchman any time."

He signed the contract, the committee rushed it to Conneaut Lake, and Greb jumped gleefully up and down like a little boy whose candy had been returned. He ran down the hill to the lake where his sparring partners were cavorting. Like an old hen he clucked and his little chicks, with busted bills, ran chirping to ma.

"Pack the bags," he yelled. "They've got Gibbons for me and we're goin' home." He socked little Patsy Scanlon on the chin, nearly tearing his head off.

It started to rain as he and Gibbons crawled through the ropes at Forbes Field a couple of weeks later. By the end of the second round the lightning was flashing, the thunder was rolling, and the water was bouncing off the canvas like marbles. Greb was a venomous cyclone, slapping, cuffing, mauling, bulling the bigger Gibbons all over the ring. He had trained for this fight and it hadn't been on green apples, hotdogs and ice cream. He had been swimming in Conneaut Lake—he was one of the few who could swim its length—running on the road and having fun with the girls. He was a ball of fire, a blockbuster and a vengeful, spiteful man all rolled into one magnificent piece of fighting machinery.

The rain poured harder, the lightning flashed oftener, the thunder rolled louder and Greb fought more ferociously as the fight progressed. Gibbons didn't relish it. He had said he could whip that Pittsburgh Dutchman any time, but he wasn't doing it this time. Coming out of a clinch, he glanced at the referee.

"Stop it!" he said curtly. "I can't fight in this rain."

"Stop it yourself, you big bum," snapped the referee. "That's what you're in here for."

The referee wouldn't stop it, Gibbons couldn't, and the Iron City Express steamed on, rolling into the terminal with speed to spare and winning from here to there and back again.

Happy Albacker had watched the fight from a ringside seat. As Gibbons climbed out of the ring, resembling a bush that had been brushed by a cloudburst, Mr. Albacker slugged him on the jaw. Greb jumped in and pushed Mr. Albacker away.

"Cut it out, Hap," he said. "Do you want Tommy to feel he's unwelcome here?"

A spectator, having bet on Gibbons, gave vent to his disappointment in a manner that impelled Mr. Albacker to slug him. A riot ensued. Greb rushed in and broke it up.

Gibbons hadn't gone yet. He wasn't the type who runs away. Mr. Albacker was sore at that remark he had made to the Pittsburgh committee about being able to whip Greb any time. He yanked a bottle out of his hip pocket and raised it to throwing position. Greb grabbed it. Mr. Albacker squinted into it, noted it wasn't empty, touched it to his not-so-parched lips and emptied it.

"See, Hap," Greb said. "Ain't that better'n wastin' it on Tommy? He's wet enough as it is. Ha, ha, ha! Some fun, eh kid?"

Two or three years later, or in 1922 Tex Rickard was casting around for an opponent to throw at Gene Tunney, then American light-heavyweight champion. There were two outstanding men—one a knockout artist, the other a consistent winner with more colour than a rainbow. Tunney preferred the latter, feeling the former was too dangerous for him at that stage of his career. Rickard, who had learned about colour as proprietor of a saloon in the

Klondike, decided to let the two prospects fight it out, the winner to meet Tunney for the title. So he matched them for old Madison Square Garden.

Presenting, in this corner, Tommy Gibbons of St. Paul. And in this corner, Harry Greb of—well, call it Paradise Beneath the Smokestacks.

Before turning them loose, there are a few sidelights that need to be touched upon, not the least of which is the matter of the Greb Specials. A slew of them, origin Pittsburgh, chugged into Penn Station the morning before the fight. Some of the passengers aboard one of them were not fight fans and they made no bones about it. Conceive of anything as unforgivable as non-fight fans riding on a Greb Special! A number of the fans couldn't. They looked upon it as sacrilege. And someplace along the route—this was during prohibition, but there was more whisky then than now—a number of these high-feathered fans took steps to inconvenience the by-then sleeping non-fight fans. A report on their activities was turned in by the Pullman conductor at Newark and when their train reached New York twenty minutes later, railroad detectives nabbed numerous of the Specialites.

A spokesman was permitted to phone Greb, who piled out of bed and raced to the aid of his townsmen. What had his people done to bring down upon their noble domes the heavy and righteous hand of the law?

"Just having some innocent fun," one of them said.

"Innocent fun, my ass!" growled a railroad bull. "You guys threw the shoes of them passengers (non-fight fans) out of the sleeping car windows."

Another bull cut in.

"And they switched the shoes of other passengers (non-fight fans), giving some of them two left shoes and others two right shoes."

Greb admitted that his was slightly on the prankish side, March in New York hardly being barefoot weather, but he said he would straighten things out if the detectives would take him to the cars where the non-fight fans were marooned, waiting to be shod. They took him. He pleaded forgiveness of his pals on the ground that they had partaken of too much, prohibition giggle water.

"If you'll drop all charges," he said, looking his sweetest, "I'll have a shoe store deliver new shoes and I'll pay for them."

The non-fight fans agreed that this was equable and they dropped charges. After arranging for the shoes to be delivered, Greb and his prankish pals went their separate, mirthful ways. En route to his suite at the Pennsylvania, Hotel, he said he hoped they would keep out of further mischief until after the fight.

"Me and Eddie Deasy was up late last night and I can handle some rest," he said. (Eddie Deasy had bet on Greb almost from his first professional fight. Greb always bet on himself, too, and Deasy took those bets for him and put them down with the gamblers.)

Interjected a friend, "Harry, you're the only famous fighter in the business who doesn't surround himself with a large, forbidding bodyguard before a fight, cutting off all outside communication. Dempsey does it. So does Tunney. Look at you! You're bleary-eyed from loss of sleep. In a few hours you'll be in there with a guy who hates your guts, a guy who is bigger than you and who, if he wins tonight, will get a crack at Tunney's title. Why don't you shut off all telephone calls and post cops outside your door?"

Greb glanced around slyly.

"And have some skirt try to get me and can't"

"It would be one hell of a sacrifice," the friend said, "but it might be worth making for a few hours."

"Maybe so, but if you think I'm gonna make it, you're crazy."

There was every reason why he should have made it. Gibbons was a vastly improved fighter over the one he had whipped in the rain in Pittsburgh. Rugged, fast, confident, smart, he was a masterful boxer. He and Greb started boxing the Same year—1913—but he hadn't subjected his body to anything approximating the punishment Greb had. He had two good eyes, too. Greb had only one and its sight had begun to dim. More, Greb was outweighed seven and one-half pounds (Greb 163+, Gibbons 171), and he was on the short end of two-to-one betting.

Back at the hotel there was not the quiet he had hoped for. His suite was crowded with hero-worshippers, bootleggers and pugs past their prime and the atmosphere was chunky with small talk. One old warhorse said, "You're gonna flatten him tonight, ain'tcha kid?"

"How many times did Dempsey flatten you?" Greb mumbled, inferring that the warhorse had flopped to the Manassa Mauler. Greb handed him a ten-dollar bill and told him, not too abruptly, to blow.

Downstairs in the lobby Pittsburgh gamblers, who had come over to back him, were heaving chairs at the New York coterie who had refused to cover on the betting odds. Someone phoned Greb, who rushed down in his dressing gown. By then the lobby was a shambles, Pittsburgh vs. New York, with some of the boys slinging furniture from the mezzanine. Greb jumped up on a reading table and with a rapidfire assortment of epithets brought about peace and contentment. A few hours later he was in the ring with the man who only recently had knocked out twenty-one of twenty-three opponents and two years later went fifteen rounds with Dempsey beneath a broiling sun in Montana's biggest fistic financial fiasco.

First of the Milk Fund fights sponsored by Mrs. William Randolph Hearst, the Garden resembled opening night at the Met. Mr. and Mrs. Vincent Astor came in with Mr. and Mrs. Kermit Roosevelt and occupied Box 42. The William K. Vanderbilts II took another box. W. Rhinelander Stewart and some of the Dukes were there. Even Joe Humphreys, the announcer, was in tails. Some of the reporters yelled "Hello, Josephus"; plain Joe was out of keeping with his finery.

It was the first time in my day that society had turned out for a prizefight. It was a novelty. There was a lot of twittering in the press section as the flossier of the old frumps, sitting in faraway boxes and looking very humphish, turned their opera glasses on the preliminary fighters and then coyly looked around to see if they were being noticed. For the most part the remarks that followed the twitters were too ribald for inclusion even in the life story of Harry Greb.

When the Messrs. Greb and Gibbons pranced into their corners and the fight fans set up the usual pandemonium that precedes the main attraction, the press section glanced around the arena to see what the blue bloods were doing. The blue bloods weren't doing anything but looking down their lorgnettes, unaccustomed as they were to shouts of "Give it to him in the breadbasket!", "Sock him on the potato!", etc.

Humphreys introduced fighters who would appear in the same ring at future dates and then he introduced Tunney, calling him the Pride of Greenwich Village. He said Tunney would box the winner of the stellar attraction at a date to be announced later.

The bell rang and out of their corners wheeled Greb and Gibbons, disrespect in their eyes, fury in their hearts, murder in their fists. It was New York's first view of them and it watched amazed while at intervals first one and then the other stepped back and spat out blood and/or teeth. The fight was featured by rough tactics, at which Greb was the aggressor and the more adept.

Tunney had said he wanted to box Greb because Gibbons, an almost technically perfect boxer as well as a knockout artist, was too experienced for him. He sat in a ringside seat, not missing a thing up there under those strong lights, and his face was somber as Greb larruped Gibbons with jarring blows from every angle and bullied him around the ring. They were talking in the clinches. I couldn't hear what they were saying, but of one thing I was sure; they weren't chanting a lullaby or repeating the Sermon on the Mount. I couldn't help notice the disapproving nods that passed between some of the stiffer old dolls of the Social Register.

It was a hard, mean fight. It was one-sided, with Greb winning twelve of the fifteen rounds, but it was vicious and frightening. Gibbons had entered the ring such a heavy favourite that not even the Pittsburgh millions could knock down the odds which in some quarters were as high as four to one. He fought hard to justify those odds. But Greb fought harder to ridicule them. He had bet his share of the purse, $17,500, on himself to win. That was the way he had always bet and that was why those Pittsburgh millions rode on his nose. When that impish gentleman poked his head through the ropes, he was mindful of his backers and his heart said no to anything short of victory.

Eddie Deasy looked up as Greb stood in his corner waiting for Humphreys to collect the verdicts of the judges and referee.

"Tommy couldn't even hit you here," said Mr. Deasy, slapping his behind with a heavy, resounding hand.

"I didn't turn it around for him," Greb said.

The New York Times covered the fight more from the social than boxing angle. The lead said Greb had won in something of an upset. Then for more than a column, save for sketchy references to the contest, it named important Social Registerites who had attended, even describing the clothes some of them wore. Mrs. Astor wore a dark dress and over it a wrap trimmed with gray squirrel. Mrs. Vanderbilt, on the opposite side of the ring, was in black with a necklace of green jade.

Havey Boyle, Pittsburgh sports columnist and for twenty years Western Pennsylvania boxing commissioner, noted this coverage and wondered why The Times hadn't mentioned that "Mr. Harry Greb of Pittsburgh was divine in green silk fighting trunks which several times during the evening threatened to slide off his rump."

Back in Pittsburgh two days later a member of Greb's party seemed to be missing. No one was sure who it was until someone asked, "Where's Eddie Deasy"

In a matter of minutes it was a refrain. In hotel lobbies, speakeasies, horse parlours and where-not, the word on everybody's lips was, "Where's Eddie Deasy."

No one had the answer. A search of his other haunts did not turn up Mr. Deasy. He was a clever man with the bottle, a fact that many were quick to admit, but not so clever, off past performances, as to drop out of sight without leaving some trace.

Greb was Still in New York. Reached by long distance, he was told Mr. Deasy was nowhere to be found. He got the manager of the Pennsylvania Hotel on the phone.

"Eddie Deasy is lost," he said. "Have you seen him around the hotel ?"

The manager said he hadn't, but that he would institute a search and report on his findings. Presently he called back.

"I found Mr. Deasy asleep in his bathtub, where, from appearances, he has been resting since the fight. What disposition do you wish made?"

"If he gets tired of that tub," Greb said, "give him another tub. He's my pal. Treat him good."

He phoned Mr. Deasy's friends in Pittsburgh, putting their troubled minds at ease, and thus ended the all-consuming "Where's Eddie Deasy?" refrain.

Greb played a return engagement at the old Garden a few months later and this time he was shooting at Tunney's American 175-pound title. The betting was fairly even, but before ringtime Greb was the two-to-one favourite. Plenty of those Greb Specials had rattled in from Pittsburgh and their financial weight had asserted itself.

Greb was not much for making pre-fight statements. He would make them to his friends and he wouldn't hedge if he had been wrong, but he didn't believe in expressing himself publicly. He made an exception this time, however, allowing that he would lift Tunney's title and punch him full of holes in the process. New York gamblers suddenly remembered what he had done to the highly touted Gibbons and they took him at his word.

For this fight he came in at 162, against 174+ for Tunney. His frame was beginning to creak under the strain of nine years of savage ring warfare mostly against opponents who outweighed him from twenty to fifty pounds, and the sight in his good eye was getting dimmer. An even worse handicap was the whispered threat that he would be thrown out of the ring if he roughed Tunney as he had Gibbons.

Tunney, on the other hand, was young and strong and coming along. He had seen Greb fight and he thought he had what it took to bring him down—patience, and a right jolt to the heart, which he practised assiduously in the training ring. It was sound logic, but he never got a, chance to use it against the wily Greb, who, before the clang of the gong had died in the opening round, rushed him to close quarters and upset his plans.

It was one of the bloodiest and most one-sided championship fights ever seen in the professional ring. Save for the third, fourth and seventh rounds, in which Tunney held his own, Greb couldn't have won more decisively if he had knocked him out a, dozen times. With the first flurry of punches, delivered before the bout was twenty seconds old, he broke Tunney's nose in two places. A moment later Tunney's face was drenched in blood and, fed by a long, ugly gash which Greb opened above his left eye it remained that way throughout the fight. Greb's gloves were soggy from slushing in the blood. The blood and sweat, like grease, were deflecting his punches. He would step back and hold out his gloves and blood-bespattered Kid McPartland, the referee, would wipe them off with a towel.

Tunney fought back gamely, doggedly moving forward. He wouldn't quit. He was a champion and the kind of champion he was doesn't know how to quit. Greb would rain a fusillade of blows against his face, down which blood cascaded, then push him away and ask McPartland, "Wanna stop it?" McPartland would ask Tunney how about it and Tunney would say, "Don't you stop it"; sometimes, when his throat was clogged with blood and he couldn't talk, he would shake his head no. Greb would leap in and resume the carnage. He would slam Tunney into the ropes and smash him with knife-sharp blows to body and head, and it was awful to watch. In almost every one of those frightful rounds he would either push Tunney away or move away himself and hold his blood-soaked gloves out. McPartland would wipe them off—he must have used half a dozen towels "and Greb would say,'Wanna stop it?" McPartland would look at Tunney and Tunney-would say, "Don't you stop it." McPartland would shake his head futilely, as much as to say, "If this man doesn't know when he's whipped, it's not for me to interfere." Then he would move from between the fighters and Greb would leap to the attack. His fists, like leather-encased bludgeons, would thud against Tunney's face, down which streamed blood not only from his left but from another gash above his right eye, and McPartland, whose clothes were bloodcaked, would duck to avoid further splashing.

Weak from the killing, relentless pace, Tunney would wipe with his forearms the blood that was blinding his eyes as it flowed into them from those open wounds, stumble into the ropes, and paw weakly at his tormenter with arms that were heavy, aching, leaden things. He smiled, too. It was a tired, half smile—the smile his fellow Marines flashed as their Jap captors kicked them and clubbed them on that bestial Death March of Bataan—but it was disdainful and it said, "I'm the champion and if you want my title you'll have to fight me until I'm incapable of defending it."

No one knew better than Greb what Tunney was thinking. He knew he would not surrender until he could no longer stand, and as long as he could do this he could hold his hands up, if only in semblance of protection. If a title had not rested on his decision McPartland would surely have stopped the uneven contest. But a referee with a heart will think hard when a champion is unflinchingly taking a beating and pleading with him not to interfere.

There was no other course for Greb than to try to pummel Tunney into submission, or, failing this, to beat him so thoroughly as to leave no doubt in the minds of boxing officials who had won. So when Tunney staggered into the ropes Greb went close and pounded him until he had to retreat or be obliterated. Following one of these manoeuvres Whitey Bimstein, who later was to second Greb against Tunney and then Tunney against Greb, slipped into the press section. He had seconded a boy in an early preliminary and now he was a spectator.

"Cute," he said of Greb's work in close, "awful cute." (Cute is ring parlance for a very wise owl, one who knows everything and never fails to press an advantage.)

At the end of fifteen brutal, terrifying rounds Greb gave Tunney over to his handlers, a bleeding, helpless hulk, and loped off with his title. Staggering uncertainly, Tunney mumbled through swollen lips, "Well, Harry, you were the better man—tonight."

"Won the championship," Greb said crisply as one of his men kissed him on his unmarked countenance and dragged him away.

Half blind, sick, his body bruised from ceaseless battering, his face a pulpy mask, Tunney stumbled toward his dressing room, blood dripping off his face onto his chest. He collapsed before he got there and his handlers carried him the rest of the way. The moment supporting hands left him, he fell back with a thud, the back of his head striking the rubbing table.

"Nature surrendered," he said.

Greb, fresh as a frisky colt, hustled uptown, rented a nightclub orchestra and danced until the musicians fell asleep.

Though nature surrendered, Tunney's heart didn't. He had taken the worst, the most sustained, beating I ever saw in any ring, yet as he lay on the rubbing table, in complete control of his mental faculties but too weak to sit up, he was recalling the fight from first to final gong. He wasn't discouraged.

"I discovered through the early part of the fight that I could whip Greb," he said. "As each round went by, battered and pummelled from post to post as I was, this discovery gradually became a positive certainty."

It was Tunney's first and only defeat—Tunney who four years later was to startle the world by dethroning the mighty and supposedly invincible Dempsey and to prove, a year later, that it was no accident by picking himself up off the floor in their return match that night in Chicago's controversial and forever-to-be-discussed Battle of the Long Count.

Twenty-three years after the first Greb-Tunney fight Happy Albacker recalled what he now refers to as the "Envelope Incident." Handed an envelope by George Engel, who managed Greb for a short time during one of Greb's squabbles with Red Mason, and told to mind it, Mr. Albacker stuffed in into his inside coat pocket and thought of it no more. Waking the next morning with the hellish uncertainty that comes from letting the hair down and kicking the heels up—and in those prohibition days the uncertainty was rugged indeed—he came up with two starts: (a) upon discovery that the envelope contained twenty thousand dollars and (b) upon being told for the first time underworld toughies had intended getting hold of that money even if they had to turn its possessor's body into a sieve with machine gun bullets.

"And there I was," Mr. Albacker sighed as he rubbed his pate, "with my belly full of tiger piddle and them hoodlums lookin' for a big frame like mine to drill some holes through. When I moaned to Greb about it his reaction made everything right: You didn't get shot, did'ja, so what'cha worryin' about, gran'ma?"

Unlike ninety-nine per cent of newly crowned champions, Greb didn't sit around waiting for promoters to come to him on bended knees. Taking to the road, he went to them, fighting wherever he could get a fight and accepting peanuts for his services if that was all some promoters could offer. That was the way it had been since he started boxing in 1913. Then, as it was always to be with him, his first question was "When am I fightin'", not "Who, and for how much?" A year before the Tunney fight, the million-faceted Billy McCarney matched him with Homer Smith in Newark, N. J. They were working on a percentage of the box-office intake. The show didn't draw, and Smith, a huge, gangling heavyweight, didn't want to go on. And George Engel wanted to call it off for Greb.

"Greb wanted to know what for," said McCarney, who because of his molasses smoothness is known throughout the universe as Professor

McCarney, "and Engel said 'Because the payoff will be in peanuts.' Greb said, 'Hell, I'll fight this tramp if all I get is the peanut bag and if the show don't draw enough to pay him, I'll pay him out'n my pocket.' "

And So he fought big Homer Smith, a foot taller and fifty pounds heavier, and he plastered him with everything in the book and plenty that wasn't. Homer got $150 for his lumps and Greb got carfare back to Pittsburgh in a day coach.

"He comes to me after the fight," Professor McCarney said, "and wants to know am I all right in the pocketbook, because if I'm not he'll kick back what little he'd got. Then in the same breath he tells me he'd have paid Smith $150 just to slap him around. You see, Greb had a score to settle with him and he settled it and everybody was happy except Homer Smith."

For the first six months after winning Tunney's American light-heavyweight title Greb engaged in over-the-weight matches in which his title was not involved, but if he had lost he no longer would have been the champion in the public's eye. One of his opponents along the trek rated himself a tough, fancy fighter, but he changed his mind after fighting Greb, from whom you could learn if you studied.

The scene in Greb's dressing room was nothing if not bedlam. Happy Albacker was cowering behind a bench and Greb was threatening to kill him if he didn't produce the following: Saint Anthony's oil and a telegram.

Mr. Albacker could understand his peevishness over the non-arrival of the Saint Anthony's oil; Greb always bathed his face in it before a fight. What he couldn't understand was the ranting about the telegram and Greb refused to elucidate. Presently a messenger came with the oil and Greb doused it on his face and forehead. Then the telegram arrived. Tearing it open, he read it aloud: "Darling, anything I have is yours for the asking."

"Greb didn't say who had sent it," Mr. Albacker said, "but I know for a fact it was not from Nicholas Murray Butler."

Greb lifted the aged messenger a foot off the floor and gaily galloped around with him. Mr. Albacker emerged from his foxhole in the dressing room. Ringtime was approaching. It was time to bandage his hands. Greb sent one of his handlers into his opponent's adjoining dressing room and his opponent returned the compliment. It is a routine function. Each fighter's observer watches the hand-taping to make sure no more tape is used than had been agreed upon and that beneath it is no plaster of Paris or other foreign substance calculated, upon contact with head or face, to do the features no particular good. These men hang around until the fighters go into the ring and it is common practice for them to put the eye on you—sometimes a hexing eye. Very often they take advantage of their mission to call you low names, the idea being to irritate you to a point that when you pile into the ring you are easy prey for their employer. These tactics were used on Greb just once. I saw the tactician not long ago and he ran screaming up Broadway at mention of Greb's name.

Greb was sitting on a stool, holding one end of the tape between his teeth. With the roll in his right hand, he was bandaging the spread-out fingers of his left. There was a knock on the door leading to the arena. He dropped the tape and it unwound across the floor as he ran over and opened the door. In strode two ladies. Before anyone realised whet was happening, he had herded his handlers and his opponent's observer into the opposition's dressing room and locked the door. While Mr., Albacker pounded frantically and emitted hysterical pleas for him to desist, he was enjoying life for which nature had so lavishly endowed him. When it was all over, he complimented the ladies on their finesse, paid them, told them that Hollywood scouts would sure as hell nab them, and sent them on their way. Then he unlocked the door to the djoining dressing room and bandaged his hands for all to see.

His opponent had lost no time during these shenanigans. He bet all the money he had with him and all he could borrow on himself to win.

"Not even Greb can get away with that stuff and beat me," he said, aware of the deleterious effect of this sort of extracurricular activity.

It was a ten-round fight. Greb was never more glorious. He hit him with everything but grandmother's bustle. He jumped at him the way you would go boo and jump at a kid you wanted to scare. The poor man jerkily threw his arms around his head and hid like an ostrich. When Greb got arm-weary from the continuous pounding he pushed him away in an I'm-through-with-You-for-the-moment attitude. The pace he set was so sizzling that several times his Flabbergasted opponent incongruously pawed furiously at the emptiness in front of him while Greb, chasing him, hit him in the back. It was so one-sided that, although it was in a city in which Greb's popularity was conspicuous by its absence, he won the unanimous decision.

"My pal atomic-bombed him," said Mr. Albacker recalling that mad, wonderful evening of the long ago. "He laid him waste, Hiroshima-ed him, never giving him time to straighten up and toss a punch from a balanced position."

Greb's first defence of his American light-heavyweight title was in old Madison Square Garden against Tommy Loughran, religious, handsome, young, ambitious, courageous, the epitome of clean living. Known as the Phantom of Philly, he held the world's light-heavyweight championship from 1927 until 1929, when he resigned it to campaign as a full-fledged heavyweight. He was one of the most polished boxers of all time. He couldn't knock your hat off, as they sag of his type of light hitter, but he was so defensively clever that you couldn't knock his off either, unless, of course, your name was Greb.

Loughran's admirers followed him from Philadelphia in Loughran Specials and were rash enough to attempt to establish him the favourite. Greb's admirers came in on Greb Specials. The two contingents met in the vicinity of Penn Station, the Pittsburghers carrying sacks of gold, lead pipes and brass knuckles, and when their hero scrambled into the ring at ten o'clock that night in 1923 Greb was the prohibitive favourite.

His work wasn't up to standard in the first three rounds, which he lost. But he found himself in the fourth and from there in it was Greb at his best. In the clinches, he used his head as a battering ram and held with one hand while he hit with the other. On the breakaways, he used his shoulders and elbows. He won ten of the fifteen rounds in a manner that left no doubt even in the minds of the Philadelphians and sent Loughran home to his people with a broken heart and without Greb's title.

That was January 30, 1923. Greb was due back in the Garden for an important engagement February twenty-third. It was too long for him to hold still. Pal Reed desired entanglements with him. Obligingly, on February fifth, Greb skipped across the Hudson to Newark and in a twelve-round non-title fight cluttered up his visage with enough leather to start a chain of tanneries. Up in Syracuse, Young Fisher had been making large waves in the pugilistic pond. Greb ankled up there on February seventeenth and in another twelve-round non-title fight reduced him to a ripple-maker,

There were still five days separating him from his Garden appearance. Red Mason, back in Greb's favour again, had to resort to every trick in the managerial bag to restrain him from going to Montreal to box the hard-hitting Soldier Jones, whose long, lean frame stood above Greb's like the Tower of Babel. Greb was furious and threatened to fire Mason, but nothing untoward happened and in exactly twenty-four nights after putting his title on the line against Loughran, he risked it against Tunney.

New Yorkers hadn't forgiven Greb for his rout of their native son in that bloody brawl nine months before and they omitted not a shade of the Bronx cheer as, his black hair combed tightly against his head and glistening with stickum, he hopped into the ring. He didn't like those boos, but he had heard them before. He had heard them all the way from London to San Francisco, and in the big and small towns and at whistle stops in-between. He fought anybody anywhere and for any amount. Three days after whipping Gibbons that time in the rain and getting seven thousand dollars for the pleasure, he scooted down to Wheeling and shellacked Greek K. O. Brown for fifty. And Greek K. O. Brown was a "snuffer" who could chill you with a punch.

The second Greb-Tunney fight was one of the most bitterly fought contests since the then-recent legalization of boxing in New York state. Greb was doing everything to Tunney, who was handling the situation commendably. Among other fouls—and he was steeped in every one in the book—he was using his thumbs which, on their way to Tunney's eyes, resembled a, leader duck in flight. From the sixth through the eleventh round he gave him fits, worrying him with a relentless, baffling attack, plunging at him, harrying him with an unorthodoxy such as the brilliant, analytical Tunney was at a loss to solve. So flagrantly did he violate the rules that Patsy Haley, the referee, stepped between them in the eighth and told Greb to behave or else. Greb told him to kiss his ass. They stood there fuming at each other while Tunney moved back and caught his breath. At the end of the twelfth Haley followed Greb to his corner and threatened him with disqualification.

Turning his back to Haley, Greb said to Red Mason, "Did'ja hear what this two-bit pimp said about heavin' me out'n the ring I'll turn him inside out if he tries it."

Meantime, the boos by the New Yorkers and the answering boos by the Pittsburghers were deafening. One reporter said, "If I get out of here without falling apart I'll never cover another Greb fight. I can't stand the excitement." A colleague had his head under the ring and was peering at the glut of wires. When I asked him what he was looking for he said, "A safer place to squat in case the booers get out of hand."

Mason's performance as a second was almost as revealing as was Greb's while fighting. As a round was about to end he took an enormous swig from the water bottle and held it in ballooned cheeks that made him look like an ogre. When the round ended he jumped into the ring and went pfuff, squirting Greb in the face and half strangling him. Sometimes Greb tried to duck, but it was no use. Mason was a Dead-Eye Dick, a human water hose with a Norden bomb sight.

Tunney got the decision of the referee and one of the two judges at the end of fifteen vicious, bruising rounds, regaining the American light-heavyweight title. Hell broke loose between New York's anti-Greb and Pittsburgh's pro-Greb element. There were no deaths, but the way noggins were being cracked there should have been.

Leaving the ring, unmarked but tired, Greb wasn't even accorded by the New Yorkers the reception with which they usually greet fallen champions. I thought he had won, and Tunney said "No one was as surprised as I was when Joe Humphreys lifted my hand in token of victory." William Muldoon, then chairman of the New York State Athletic Commission, was even more surprised. "The decision in Tunney's favour," he said, "was unjustifiable." There was talk of a reversal, but Muldoon stood by the decision of his subordinates.

Greb was mad as a hornet but, after castigating Haley and the judges, he took it philosophically, lauded Tunney on his courage and improvement and went out and had a good time. His wife, Mildred, semi-invalided from tuberculosis, died a short time later and friends said worry over the loss of his title had hastened the end.

Greb felt so good wearing a pugilistic crown, and it fitted his regal head so perfectly, that he stepped out and plucked himself off another one, the middleweight. To withhold the circumstances under which he got the fight that made him twice a champion would be an unpardonable omission.

Johnny Wilson had held the title three years. He had seen Greb fight many times and what he craved was as little proximity as possible. He could buy poison at any drug store and in any amount, so why take an overdose by climbing into the ring with that cantankerous man with the devil's lash in his hands?

Cognizant of Wilson's shyness, Greb took steps. Corralling waiters at Pittsburgh's then Motor Square Hotel, now the Ritz, he outlined his scheme. It simmered down to this: the waiters would serve him coloured water in a whiskey glass, Greb would rapidly guzzle it down and fall asleep in a drunken stupor. All parties concerned shook hands on the proposition, promptly putting it into effect. That's how it got around that Greb was a booze hound. But he wasn't a booze hound, he was a girl hound and it took a fleet dear to outdistance him once he lit out after her.

He not only saw to it that Wilson's manager, Marty Killelea, heard about his debauchery but actually saw it with his own appraising eyes. From Pittsburgh he converged on New York, repeating his strategy at Jimmy Kelly's and other night spots where a favoured customer could sneak a drink during the heyday of Pussyfoot Johnson, prohibition's busybody sleuth. Practically overnight it got abroad that he was drinking himself silly over the loss of his title to Tunney. No doubt about it, he was ready for the cleaners. Impatiently, Wilson signed for the defence of his middleweight title before some other fighter was catapulted into the headlines by slaying the hollow shell that was now Greb, and bing, bang, bing! he didn't have it any more.

Resembling nothing so much as a perpetual motion machine gone berserk, Greb was not particularly disturbed with the manner in which he landed blows. He butted nicely in the clinches, too, and hit effectively on the breakaways. He drew warnings for his playful pastime of knubbing with his gloved fist when the thumb was extended. And once, when his left thumb was engaged in excavating Wilson's right eye, Jack O'Sullivan, the referee, pushed him away and asked him what he thought he was doing. "Gouging Johnny in the eye, can't you see?" Greb said haughtily.

By this time Wilson himself had become disdainful of the niceties of the accepted rules of ring warfare and he was rougher than a grizzly bear. Fearful that he might lay a haymaker left on Greb's chin, Red Mason ambled over to the knockdown timekeeper with a water bottle in his hand.

"What's he doing over there?" asked a reporter sitting next to me. It was a sixty-four dollar question, but anyone who knew Mason could supply the answer.

"You'll see," I said, "If Wilson happens to drop Greb, Mr. Mason will whang the gong—and the knockdown timekeeper too if necessary—with the bottle, thus ending the round prematurely and giving him a chance to revive his innocent little lamb before the next round comes up."

"Innocent little lamb!" the reporter said in a low, confidential voice. "Greb is an Indian uprising."

But Mason didn't have to whang the gong. Greb won thirteen of the fifteen rounds, leaving behind him a former middleweight champion with a large cut on the bridge of his long snout, bleeding and torn mouth into which a yanking thumb had been dropped, puffed and raw lips, his left eye almost closed and a lump under his right eye the shape of a zeppelin and almost as big. Greb was spitting blood, but there were no marks on his cute, owlish face.

The Messrs. Greb and Eddie Deasy and numerous of their friends scampered back to Pittsburgh with so much money that they had to bury it until Andy Mellon could throw up a new bank big enough to hold their winnings.

Greb gave Wilson a, chance to regain the title five and a half months later and the only difference between this and the first encounter was that Greb wasn't bleeding from the mouth when it was all over.

Tex Rickard knew a smart match without consulting the crystal ball. "Never seed nothin' like it," he drawled.

It wasn't often then—and it is almost unheard of now—that two great champions went to the barrier against each other.

Accordingly, three months and ten days after destroying Wilson on August 31, 1923, Greb was back in the old Garden against Tunney, with Tunney's 175-pound, but not Greb's 160-pound, title the lure. Two hours before the opening preliminary policemen were having their hands full keeping the crowd in line at the ticket windows. The fans knew they weren't going to be bored with a couple of fancy, posturing, powder-puff punchers. They knew, too, that sections of those Greb Specials had been thundering across the Alleghenies during the day and night and that in their cargoes was dynamite—dynamite, money, heart, and that all of these would be behind their warrior from the city whence the sometimes too-turbulent Ohio begins its snaky way.

Joe Humphreys introduced the usual number of ring celebrities, of whom Battling Siki was far and away the most colourful. Called by Runyon the Singular Senegalese, this amiable Negro from the African jungle had only recently knocked out Georges Carpentier for the world's light-heavyweight title in Paris and then added to that prestige by darting in and out of Montmartre pleasure houses with a tiger on a leash. Even more recently he had naively gone to Dublin, where, on St. Patrick's Day, he dropped the title to Michael McTigue.

It was fifteen minutes from the time Siki left his roost in Peanut Heaven, where for two hours his noisy Harlem admirers had been calling the crowd's attention to him, before he reached the ring. Smiling toothily like a child contemplating a lollipop, he was wearing brogans, skintight pants, tails and topper and carrying a cane. After bowing all over the ring, he leaned against the ropes, slipped in a pool of blood from one of the preliminaries and started to tumble out of the ring. Irish Johnny Curtin, a good Jersey City bantamweight, grabbed him and pulled him back in. Greb and Tunny sat in their corners, bored with all the hoop-la and itching to earn their night's pay. Obviously drunk, Siki went over to Tunney and tried to kiss him in the French manner. Tunney ducked. He tried it on Greb and Greb ducked. He was another fifteen minutes en route to his roost, by which time he was barely a memory. Greb and Tunney had swung into action in their third fight, and when those stalwarts started swinging everything else paled by comparison.

Tunney had lost most of his timidity, Greb never had any. For fifteen mean, fast rounds they whaled each other. Retreating only when common sense said they must, they literally leaned their heads against each other's chests and fought like jealous stallions. One New York newspaper referred to them as the new Tunney and the new Greb. It called Tunney new because, whereas he had been hesitant he was now almost audacious, and Greb new because he had fought one of his cleanest fights. The referee didn't call Greb for a single foul, though I detected some careless bobbing of the head and gouging of the thumb that were reminiscent of rougher nights. The difference in this third fight was that Tunney, having profited by experience, had worked out his own formula for coping with Greb's disregard for the rules. He didn't prefer it that way, regarding boxing as a vigorous, constructive endeavour, but he meant to stay in the ring until he got out of it what he wanted. If Greb could further his interests by being careless, then was there anything wrong with Tunney's fighting carelessness with carelessness?

"Don't forget," Tunney said, "that neither my head nor my thumbs were tied down."

Still American light-heavyweight and world's middleweight champions, respectively, they fought twice again, their fourth fight in Cleveland, their fifth in St. Paul. Both were violent, no-quarter giving slug-fests so bitter in their unrelenting fury that the fans, showing no partiality, cheered first one and then the other. For the Cleveland fight Greb had gone back to his old diet of hotdogs and ice cream; green apples would have been included if there had been any around that September night in 1924. It didn't kick up on him this time and he set such a furious pace that neither he nor Tunney heard the bell ending the seventh round and the referee had difficulty prying them apart. It was a no-decision ten-rounder, the laws of Ohio prohibiting the rendering of anything but an unofficial newspaper decision. The New York Times called it a draw, adding, however, that the majority of ringside experts thought Tunney's accurate and more effective punching entitled him to the shade.

Following the St. Paul fight their fifth and last, Greb said Tunney had "carried" him.

"He broke two of my ribs," he said. "He's gettin' too big and too strong and hitting too hard. It's time for somebody else to fight him for a change. Don't let no one tell you Gene can't hit. He hit me so hard in the belly I couldn't hardly breathe. He'll whip Dempsey. Maybe he'll knock him out."

He didn't think Tunney "carried" him so much out of altruism as for business reasons. Tunney was angling for a match with Tommy Gibbons (and he got it and he knocked Gibbons out). Gibbons was a St. Paul boy. Greb reasoned, "If after what I done to Tommy Gene had knocked me out in front of his very eyes, do you think Tommy would'a give him a match?"

The recording of a short conversation with Greb following his third Tunney fight is a must. The older generation well recalls the renown Tunney came into as a Shakespearean scholar. Indeed, he lectured on this subject at Yale shortly after winning Dempsey's title in 1926

Expecting a reply none too complimentary to Tunney, I asked. Greb what he thought of Shakespeare. He gave me a quick look. "Shakespeare! How much does he weigh?"

Tunney was a greatly underrated fighter. He lacked Greb's and Dempsey's colour, but he was a cool, efficient craftsman, a damaging body puncher. He could handle a punch, too, and he was dead game. In contrast to other fighters, he preferred books and erudite friends to the fight mob. Newspapermen sometimes went out of their way to take journalistic sideswipes at him on the theory that, being a, prizefighter, how could he be as smart as he was supposed to be? How about Eddie Eagan, chairman Of the New York State Athletic Commission? A Rhodes scholar from Yale, he was captain of the American Olympic boxing team in 1924. True, he wasn't a professional, but he could have been. He boxed an exhibition with Dempsey, who didn't know how to pull his punches, and he did all right. And how about Victor McLaglen of the cinema? He fought the great Jack Johnson. Has anyone ever accused James Cagney of being a mental midget? Before he ever dreamed of socking ladies with grapefruit, much less winning an Academy Award for the-outstanding cinematic performance a few years ago, he knew what to do with a pair of boxing gloves. Then there's James Adolf Leftwich. A University of Virginia student, he was a middleweight on the Olympic team captained by Eagan. Known as the amateur Stanley Ketchel, a pugilistic name to conjure with, he is a former New York newspaperman and now one of the country's leading public relations counsels.

I never knew a great fighter who wasn't God-fearing and sentimental and who, given a chance, couldn't express himself. A case in point is an experience I had with one last October.

For nine tedious weeks I had laboured over this chapter, Thunder Over Pittsburgh, only to have it disappear in transit to my publisher. My first thoughts were of this fighter. I had seen him come from behind. Maybe a visit with him would give me courage. We had talked on the phone and he had given me data, not knowing how I might slant it to favour Greb. We had made a dinner appointment, too, but he bad had to break it because of more pressing demands on his time. The thought of writing the chapter over again, with only a few sheets of the first draft to guide me, was so unpleasant that I appealed to him for help.

"I'll be at your apartment at noon Tuesday," he said. "No matter what happens, I'll be there Tuesday."

He phoned from Grand Central Tuesday, saying he would be down in twenty minutes.

I was waiting on the sidewalk when his cab pulled up. It was the first time I had seen him when he wasn't fighting someone. Now he was the only living undefeated world's heavyweight champion, married and the father of three sons and one daughter, and had been through his second war (a Navy Commander in this one, a combat Marine in the other) .

He looked much bigger than he had looked in the ring, though actually he was within five pounds of his fighting weight when he retired nearly twenty years ago. He was wearing a Homberg hat and a conservative business suit; Greb would have worn red pants and a yellow jacket if he could have found them. There were marks of his former trade on his strong, forthright face— cuts under his chin where he had been butted, scars around and over his eyes, a slightly thick ear. Yet he had the easy hearing of an Anthony Eden. His voice was mellow as ancient wine, his words descriptive and to the point.

He knew I had hero-worshipped Greb, that I had pulled for Greb in all their fights. But that was long ago and now he had inconvenienced himself to befriend his dead conqueror's pal. We talked about everything except Greb and the loss of Thunder Over Pittsburgh. Suddenly I asked, "Did Harry thumb you?"

He looked at me for half a minute and then in a low voice at once reverent he said, "Yes, he thumbed me. He butted me. He tried to kill me. The moment we signed for a fight he was my enemy and he detested me. But after a fight it was a different matter and it remained that way until we were matched again. If ever an athlete deserved a monument to his greatness, to his endurance, to his sportsmanship, it was Harry Greb. Anything he did to you—and he did everything he could to dismember you-you could do back to him and he wouldn't complain."

When he talked of unfairness—and this fighter had been on the receiving end of plenty of it—his kindly, sharp eyes changed quickly to a, fighter's eyes and they were cold as steel.

Twice he had fought the truculent but sportive Chuck Wiggins, one of whose classic ring performances with Greb was set down for posterity a few chapters back. I told him about their gentleman's agreement that night in Grand Rapids whereby they forswore unnecessarily roughhouse tactics, got memory lapses during the heat of battle, and ended up in a brawl in which Greb bit a hunk out of Chuck's nose.

He said he had wondered, as he was boxing Wiggins, by what unhappy circumstances he had come by that hole in his trumpet. It reminded him of an amusing incident.

"I was boxing Wiggins in Boston," he said. "I was developing a new punch. After feinting, I would bend down, slip in, and bring a left uppercut to the solar plexus or liver. My judgment of distance was not yet good. On two occasions I tried this on Chuck, and was cautioned by the referee both times for hitting low. In the seventh round, I slipped in again and accidentally hit Chuck low. The referee jumped between us, ready to give the fight to Chuck on a foul, but Chuck pushed him aside—he wouldn't take a fight on a foul unless he was incapacitated—and said, 'Christ, Gene, no kidding, that was low ! Keep 'em up!' "

Here, then, is Gene Tunney writing about his five bitter Greb fights in his book Arms For Living, published a few years ago.

"Few human beings have fought each other more savagely or more often than Harry Greb and I. We punched and cut and bruised each other in a series of bouts, five of them. The first of the five is for me an enduring memory, a memory still terrifying.

"I was in bad shape for the bout. This was in the time when my hands were chronically ailing with imperfectly mended fractures, sore and swollen. In my dressing room before going into the ring Novocaine was shot into them to deaden the pain that would ensue upon striking blows. Moreover, I had above my left eye a half-healed cut sustained in training. Adrenaline chloride was injected into the eyebrow to prevent the cut from bleeding too much if reopened by Greb's punches. Then the bout started and the nightmare began....

"In the first exchange of the fight, I sustained a double fracture of the nose which bled continually...Toward the end of the first round, my left eyebrow was laid open four inches. In the third another cut over the right eye left me looking through a red film. For the better part of twelve rounds I saw a red phantom-like form dancing before me.

"It is impossible to describe the bloodiness of this fight. How I ever survived the thirteenth, fourteenth and fifteenth rounds is still a mystery to me.

"All five of our fights were of that order of savagery. My showing became better from one to another—and in the last bout I beat Harry about as badly as he had beaten me in the first. The ferocity of the hammering Greb took is indicated by a remark he made toward the end. In a clinch he said, 'Gene, don't knock me out!'

"That from Harry Greb was monumental. No one was gamer. Pain and punches meant nothing to him—the cruel mauling, the bruising punishment. But Harry, hopelessly beaten, didn't want the folks back home to read that he had been knocked out. I was never paid a higher tribute, Here was one of the gamest and greatest fighters of all time laying down his shield, admitting defeat and knowing that I would not expose him....

"Greb was curiously secretive in pride, oddly vain. He was concerned about his looks. Strange that anyone so careful of his face should have selected prizefighting for a profession. When tough Harry Greb went to one of the roughhouse, slugging brawls for which he was famous, he took with him not merely his pugilistic equipment, trunks, bathrobe, ring shoes! Invariably he carried along a comb and brush, mirror, and—marvel at it—a powder puff! Going into the ferocious fracas, he always had his hair plastered down with stickum. This was one of the strangest eccentricities I ever observed in the realm where fists thud into the human visage

"Harry Greb's vanity about his looks cost him his life. Retiring from the ring with a substantial and hard-earned fortune, his first concern was his nose, flat and shapeless from countless punches and repeated fractures. Like an aging society beauty, he resorted to plastic surgery. He died on the operating table while his nose was being made shapely.

"Harry was bitter about one fight, our fourth. I won the decision, and this enraged him. He was sure he had beaten me, felt to the depth of his soul that he had been the victor. It was a newspaper decision affair of the period, sports writers giving the verdict in their stories. Regis Welsh of the Pittsburgh Post was one of Greb's best friends. In his account of the battle, he gave the decision to me. He put my photo on the front page with the caption 'Too much for our boy.'

"All the bitterness the battle had stirred in Greb was directed not against me, not against the antagonist who had been in there hitting him, but against his newspaper friends who had merely typed a few keys on a typewriter. He didn't resent the physical pain of being murdered; he resented losing unjustly, as he thought. His sense of right was touched, and his vanity. He and I remained the best of friends, with never the slightest bit of anger or ill will.

"I like to recall the attitude of Harry Greb. Harry was refreshing. In the savage battles we had fought I had gained his respect. When told that I read books, Greb replied,'You're crazy.' He simply wouldn't believe it, and that's all there was to it—'You're crazy!' "

Chapter VIII

Sheik of Charleroi

The elevator stopped at the ninth floor of Cathedral Mansions. Apartments in the lovely Schenley district of Pittsburgh and the operator nodded toward a door that was ajar.

"That's his apartment," he said warmly. "Swellest little dude in town. Go right in, he's expectin' you."

There was a baby carriage outside the door and from inside came these low, throaty, sing-song words: "Pappa will take C. O. D. to London, to Paree, to Australia, to New Zealand, to Mehico City...."

As I stood there I couldn't help reflecting on the first time I had ever seen this little dude who was calling himself pappa. He was roughly eighteen, with sideburns that came down to his earlobes, and he was wearing bell-bottom trousers whose waist reached almost to his armpits. He came to Greb's manager, Red Mason, and said he was forsaking amateur boxing and was turning pro and asked Mason to handle him.

"A little sheik!" Mason said in a voice only semi-friendly.

"Sheik of Charleroi (Pennsylvania) is what they call me."

"Get your clothes off and let's see what you've got." Mason handed him big, heavily padded gloves and boxing trunks and gave him a hard eye—an eye that said, "Listen, fresh guy, your cockiness is exceeded only by your ignorance. You'll see."

Ten minutes later, dressed for the test, the little man stood outside the training ring in which a cyclone was ripping.

"Mister Greb, I presume," he said, lifting his eyebrows and pursing his lips in a most disconcerting manner.

"You won't be presuming very long," Mason said frigidly, "and you won't be calling him Mister, either. Get in there and let's see if you've got a pro's heart."

He got in there, and Greb banged into him, and in less than ten minutes everybody knew that he had a pro's heart.

It had been a long time since I had seen him, but I knew as I stood there with my memories, that he was speaking with authority about all those places of which he was telling C. O. D., because he had fought in them. Now he had retired from the profession in which he had made half a million dollars only to be wiped out of everything he owned during the depth of the depression and at the end, for him, of the pugilistic trail.

I pushed the door open.

"Lives here the Sheik of Charleroi?"

"Not the boo-ti-ful man of yesteryear," he answered, running out to greet me, "but otherwise the same little Dago."

Dago ! That was what Greb used to call him, sometimes with deep undertones of affection, sometimes the reverse. Recalling it, he moved his hand over his nose, then over his right ear, then over and around his eyes.

"See these?" Battered nose, thick ear, cuts around his eyes.

A lot of leather had been leaned against his once handsome face since that afternoon nearly twenty-five years ago when Red Mason had come down off his high horse and -stabled him with Greb.

"A lot," he admitted, "and all the way from Singapore to New York and back again. But it was that old debbil Greb who gave me these lumps."

Over by the kitchen was a play pen and in it a robust, happy baby naked save for a diaper.

"C. O. D.?" I ventured.

"Charles Oliver DeMarco," said the sire proudly. "Notice that big diaper he's wearing' He's got the biggest can of any kid his age in Pittsburgh."

"For a baby," I said, "big back muscles, too. Incidentally, I hear he's the new bouncer at the Continental Bar."

"Pacifier," he corrected airily. "Bouncer suggests violence."

If ever anybody knew about violence it was this man. I've mentioned him elsewhere in these pages, but you can't dismiss that quickly the man who in 1925 fought sixty-seven fights, topping by fourteen Johnny Dundee's unofficial fifty-three, and who participated in three hundred eighty-three, a near record, before he quit the ring in 1932.

"Ruth," Cuddy DeMarco called affectionately to his wife, "drop 'at mop and come in here and meet my old colleague."

A private secretary before her marriage, Mrs. DeMarco came in from the kitchen in which she was cooking a spaghetti dinner.

"You haven't seen Cuddy for a long time," she said. "Has he changed much, and do you think he's punch drunk?"

"Anything but," I said. "He's busted up around the face, all right, but the bells are clear upstairs."

"I feel just like a boy," Cuddy said. "The tick is rhythmical. too, eh Jim?"

"Has anyone ever indicated it wasn't?"

"There have been whispers," his wife said.

"Any of the great trainers Whitey Bimstein, Ray Arcel—will dispel them. They'll tell you that in all their association with fighters they've never known a mentally alert One whose mind has been affected, no matter how much he has been hit on the chin. It's only the plodding slow thinkers who get bats in the belfry."

"Indirectly," Cuddy said, "word comes to me that my voice sounds as if it's coming out of a well. It wasn't that way before. What caused it?"

"Punches around and on the Adam's apple will do it. They impair the nerves of the voice box."

Pointing again to his scars and reiterating it was that old debbil Greb who gave them to him in the training ring, Cuddy said, "But I'm not hurt. (Fighters abhor such expressions as punch-drunk, slaphappy, etc., and when the smart ones refer to what technically is known as ataxic aphasia, they say hurt.) Slapsie Maxie Rosenbloom isn't hurt, is he? He took an awful biffing around by Greb many semesters ago in Cleveland and after reading about him and seeing him in pictures I sometimes wonder if maybe he caught a few too many on the chops."

"I've been told by people who know," I said, "that that's his normal condition."

In the DeMarco kitchen, where we had dinner, a glass jar full of paper-wrapped pennies sat on a shelf by the table.

"C. O. D.'s," Cuddy said. "He gets all the pennies. And I've taken out an annuity that guarantees him a college education."

Mrs. DeMarco said, "You know Cuddy lost his fortune during the depression. By then he was too old to fight, but he always was a busy little bee anyhow, so he started selling things. He sells almost everything under the sun—hardware, horses and saddles, second-hand autos, sports goods, glassware, cutlery and all kinds of men's furnishings. Senator Joe Guffey, former Governor Earle and Dick Mellon (Richard K. Mellon, president of the Mellon National Bank) buy suits from him. Tell Jim about Mr. Mellon."

"Retiring to the point of shyness, but a very fine chappie—aye aye, a very fine chappie, old man," Cuddy said, parading the accent he had picked up when he was in England teaching their pugs some of the finer points of the Manly Art of Modified Murder. "The only..."

"You see," Mrs. DeMarco interrupted, "it's that accent that makes people wonder. C. O. D. will be aping him pretty soon and then people'll think they're both tetched. Go ahead, Cuddy, and finish about Mr. Mellon."

"The only time I see him is at his bank—the most beautiful bank in the world. I look into my crystal ball and it tells me he's in the market for a suit. When the girl ushers me into his office, he says, 'Why, hello there, Cuddy. Glad to see you. You've got a bloodhound's nose; I need a suit.' I whip out my samples, he selects one of them and I call my tailor in and get his measurements. You would never suspect it, but Mr. Mellon is a clever boxer and a stiff, accurate left hooker. He could give a lot of preliminary boys trouble for a couple of rounds."

Cuddy DeMarco was a Ripley Believe-It-Or-Not fighter. Weighing someplace between 118 and 125 pounds in his prime, he fought five champions—all the way up the line to and including welterweights—and he whipped them, but he never held a title. To get these matches he had to post sizable forfeits as guarantees he would enter the ring heavier than the title limit. If he won, all he got out of it (plus, of course, his end of the purse) was the satisfaction; his opponents' titles remained intact. Most of the time he couldn't pack on the necessary heft. That was when Red Mason took over. Glib as a rooster at dawn, he entertained boxing officials with stories, sometimes dramatic, sometimes pointless, sometimes hilarious—depending on his estimate of his listeners' intelligence—and he fixed the scales in front of their sharp, distrusting eyes. When Cuddy's weight would be announced as, say, 148, or one pound above the welterweight title poundage, Mason would squeal, "Cripes, Cud, you're fatter'n a hawg." Actually, Cuddy was so thin that two of him could get into a thimble and there would still he room for a light housekeeping unit.

"But none of those men ever messed me up,'" Cuddy said: "It was that old debbil Greb. He was the fastest man I ever saw in the ring—fast on his feet and with his hands. And you couldn't out-guess him. He was always thinking ahead of you. If you tried to feint him, he hit you before you could give him the deceptive eye. I feinted Billy Petrolle and Louis Kid Kaplan and Joe Dundee all over the ring and drove them crazy, but every time I tried it on Greb during the hundreds of times I trained with him, he knocked me on my can."

With the possible exception Of Johnny Ray, developer and manager of Billy Conn, Cuddy was the only one of Greb's many stablemates who day after day could stand up under the drubbings to which he subjected them. But Greb and Ray, one of the classiest lightweights I ever saw, feuded so much that Red Mason, fearful of the damage they might inflict, seldom permitted them to work out together. It was little Cuddy (with many assists from the even tinier Patsy Scanlon) upon whom the fistic hand of fate fell when Greb was pressed for a sparring partner who could give him the competition he had to have in preparation for an important fight.

They were at dagger's point half the time, but Greb, like a high-strung race horse, had to have a mascot. He didn't care for goats or any of the other animals race horses are often fond of, so Cuddy drew the assignment. They not only worked out together but lived together.

"The going was some times vigorous," Cuddy said. "And on top of it all, he was afraid to go to sleep in the dark. He feared no man. He would get up off the floor and with the most frightful display of courage imaginable kick the bejesus out of men like Dempsey, but he wouldn't go to sleep unless there was a light in the room."

Without being conscious of it, the roughhouse Greb, when he wasn't trying to decapitate him in the training ring, treated Cuddy as if he were a toy suddenly come to life. When he introduced him to a girl, an item he was seldom without, he often referred to him as Little Cuddles, forgetting that Cuddy was small, dark and handsome and as clever a word juggler as ever flattered a lady. Under Cuddy's spell, it wasn't long until the girls were cooing and saying what a darling little character he was, ignoring Greb. And it wasn't long, either, until Greb was squirming and trying, sometimes unsuccessfully, to get Cuddy's eye in a subtle effort to tell him to take to the tall timber.

"I always knew when to scram," Cuddy said, "but I didn't always heed my better judgment in time. Greb got the jump on me and he would throw me into a bathtub, lagoon, bullrush, incinerator whatever convenient place there was in which to throw me."

On a trip to Hot Springs, Arkansas, where he and Cuddy were taking the baths, Greb consented to box Mel Stevenson, or Stevens, Cuddy doesn't remember which. No point had been made of it, but it was generally understood, since Stevenson was unknown, that it would be a sort of exhibition in which Greb would demonstrate his prowess without, however, bearing down too hard. A couple of days before the bout someone asked him what kind of condition he was in.

"Not very good, Why?" Greb asked.

"Because," this man said, "Stevenson is a clever boxer and a terrific hitter. He's liable to sneak a lucky one over on you and drop you or even knock you out. You know how it would project him into the limelight and also make you look like a prize chump for taking such a chickenfeed match out here in the sticks."

Greb wasn't afraid of anything that lived, but he would listen to intelligent advice. Regardless of the circumstances, he trusted an opponent no more than MacArthur trusts the Japs. And after that Johnstown experience, detailed in a preceding chapter, he didn't even trust Cuddy. There wasn't time to get into shape for an opponent as potentially dangerous as Stevenson was supposed to be, so he said to Cuddy, "Listen, sweetheart, you fight him."

"How big is he?" Cuddy asked.

"Hundred sixty-five."

"And me, I'm not even a hundred twenty-five."

"The weight don't make no difference," said Greb, who never worried about an opponent's weight himself and couldn't understand why anyone else should. "Go ahead, Cud, and take the fight. I'll second you. If Stevenson hurts you, manoeuvre him over to your corner and pretend like you want to ask me something. The fans will be watching you, not me, and I'll belt him on the chin. Then you can knock him silly and look like a hero."

While Cuddy was trying to think of an excuse to say no without incurring the disfavour of his celebrated stablemate, Greb inundated him with persuasiveness.

"All right," Cuddy said, "I'll take the fight."

As far as he knew he would be giving away forty pounds—and this to a man the terrific Greb, a murderer even when he was out of condition, wanted no traffic with. There were times when Greb didn't seem to care what happened to his little pal. And for some strange reason he had neglected to impart the information that Stevenson was an all-round tough nut. Cuddy had heard about it, though, but he wanted to know more. He wanted to know how he fought, was he a southpaw or right-hander, a stand-up fighter or one who weaved and boxed out of a crouch, a slow starter who gathered momentum as the bout progressed or vice versa?—things a fighter must know about his opponent in advance of a fight. So he despatched a reliable scout to check up on these essentials. The report came back that Greb's data was cock-eyed. Stevenson wasn't a 165-pounder with a killing punch, as Greb had been informed, but a 150-pounder who couldn't whip his palsied great-grandmother.

For once Cuddy didn't use his head. He started to tell Greb about the soft touch-Greb who knew what you were thinking before the thought could be transferred into words.

"I been tryin' to find you, Cud," interrupted the psychic Greb, "to tell you I reconsidered. I'm takin' the fight. Even if Stevenson is a tramp which couldn't lick a postage stamp, he's too big for you and he's liable to hurt you."

"I appreciate your sudden interest in my welfare," Cuddy said with all the sarcasm at his command. "However, you turned the fight over to me and now that you know it's a, soft touch you've developed a paternal interest in my safety."

"It was only a gag, darlin'," Greb said, trying to clown. "I was only testin' your loyalty. I had no intention of lettin' you fight that big guy. He would hurt you sure as hell."

"It's mighty peculiar that you start worrying about me at this late date. How about all the times you tried to croak me in workouts?"

"Workouts," Greb said, "don't count. And besides I wouldn't hurt you for nothin' if I could help it."

"No! How about that time in Johnstown?"

This was Cuddy's second mistake. It brought back memories of the time he had dropped Greb on the seat of his pants in front of all those hero-worshippers.

Mumbling "Johnstown! Johnstown! you little Dago bastard, I'll fix you for that sneak punch," Greb lunged at him. Cuddy bolted.

"Lucky for me," he said, "that I had good eyes and he didn't. I left him so far behind on the stairs that by the time he reached the street I was lamming it in a cab."

Cuddy knew how long it took Greb to cool off. In an hour he returned to their suite.

"How about Stevenson? Am I or are you fighting him?"

"Go ahead and fight him, you little stinker," Greb muttered, "but if he hurts you I'm not gonna belt him on the chin like I promised." His attitude was that of a bad, bad boy whose motives had been examined and found wanting. But by ringtime he had forgiven himself and Cuddy, too. Actually and literally he was in his little stablemate's corner. He scampered over to Stevenson's corner after the referee's instructions.

"Cuddy's only a baby," he said icily, raking the heel of his hand down over Stevenson's nose and nearly breaking it, "and if you muss a hair in his head I'll knock you loose from your ears right here in the ring."

Cuddy hesitated and, after fumbling in his wallet, produced a photo of Greb. He looked at it a long, long time.

"Wonderful bastard, wasn't he?"

"How did you do against Stevenson?" I asked.

"Greb scared him to death and I flattened him in the third."

After dinner at the DeMarcos, we drove out to the Garfield district where Greb was born and where he lived all his life. With us were Jimmy Daugherty, a customers' man recently discharged from the army, and John Coyle, a public relations man. En route, the conversation was mostly about Cuddy's fistic contemporaries and the current crop.

"Comparison gets you nowhere," Cuddy said, "but we were more active when I was boxing. For instance, I fought four times in five nights in four different states, jumping five hundred miles for each bout."

Coyle said, "You know, I wasn't interested in Cuddy as a personality until one day I was reading a Pierce Arrow Motor Company's published list of recent purchasers. The first two names were those of Mrs. W. L. Mellon and Mrs. Frank Loevy, two of Pittsburgh's most important women. Cuddy's was the third. I said to my wife, 'Every time I see that little dude he's with a United States Senator, Governor, Federal Judge or somebody of consequence. I've gotta meet him.' "

Our first stop was at Holtz's Tavern. Two photos of Greb hung on the wall at the end of the bar. Coyle, who lives in Garfield, said "Before you open a bar out here, you get a photo of Greb, tack it up where everybody can see it, then apply for a tavern license. If it's a good photo, you get the license. If it isn't, you don't."

Greb wasn't a whiskey head and Coyle wasn't implying that he was: What he meant was that it is in the saloon where most people congregate and Greb lives in the hearts of all his old neighbours.

Billy Holtz, solemn-faced, compactly built, remembered Greb well.

"I saw Joe Louis flatten Hens Burkie here some years ago. He was a fast puncher and he had polish. What he didn't have was speed afoot and I said to myself, 'Greb would have run in on him and murdered him. Joe would have thought he was fighting a revolving, indestructible electric fan.' "

A lady drinker who had been whooping it up all evening knew Greb when he was in grade school.

"With the girls," she said, "he was the berries. I used to see him strutting down the street with them, carrying their books. When he came to a mud puddle he would pick them up and carry them over it with gusto. If other boys approached, Greb butted them off the sidewalk like a billygoat."

A retired bricklayer said he had seen every one of Greb's Pittsburgh fights from the time he started as a pro. He took a frayed Runyon column out of his card case and, explaining that he was supplying his own transitions, quoted the following:

"The kind of guy I like is a knock-down-drag-out ring fighter... a lunging, plunging, rip-snorter.. slam-bang slugger, all movement and action from head to toe, of fighting fury so intense as to cause him to forget the rules, the officials, the bell, and everything but the business at hand." He folded the column carefully and put it back in the card case.

"Greb was that kind of fighter," he said. "The cards were stacked against him the night he fought Al McCoy here at the old Exposition Building at the Point. McCoy brought his own referee. Greb's manager tried to nix this deal, but Greb wouldn't let him. Long before the fight was over Greb was fighting both McCoy and his private referee and he sent them to the cleaners. He was a fury fighter who never let you down and that's why we'll never forget him."

Solidly slung together was a squat man who said he was a truck driver.

"I never see nothin' like Greb. He was a tom-cat. Before a fight, when other fighters was takin' it easy, he was bustin' 'round with the petticoats, and after a fight it was the same thing. Christ, that guy had more juice in one night than I got in a month o' Sundays, and me I'm healthy like a bull." He pounded his chest rapturously, and his woman companion said there was no doubt about it, he was healthy.

A bus driver had gone to school with Greb and grown up with him. "His only weakness," he said, "was girls, and I'm weak that way but not as capable. I saw him in all his fights here. When I see a ring I can't help but think he will climb up there and lambast the daylights out of somebody, but I know he's not going to, so I haven't gone to no more than two fights since Harry died."

A precise, smallish old man well versed in fistic terms had known Greb all his life. He saw him fight Ted (Kid) Graves, clever welterweight champion, in the Power House, Pittsburgh, early in his career.

"Harry broke his left forearm in the first round, but won the second before he had to quit in his corner. When he took his arm out of the splint it was just enough crooked to turn an ordinary jab into a halfhook. Harry said 'It was one of the best breaks of my career.'"

Everywhere we went there was complete agreement on these points; Greb would rather do either of two things than eat and one of them was fight.

Little more than a stone's throw from Garfield is Lawrenceville, home of the five fighting Zivics. Two of them, Pete and Jack, were contemporaneous with Greb. There has been a Zivic in the ring for the last twenty-five years. Fritzie was the most successful. In 1940 he dethroned Henry Armstrong for the world's welterweight crown, last of the three titles simultaneously held by that slam-bang Negro from California. Henry thought it was an accident, or that the boxing officials were blind, or that he had had an off night. Would Fritzie give him a return bout?

"Any time, Henry," Fritzie said as he hopped a train for Washington, where, in his first public statement since zooming into international prominence, he practically assured Wendell Willkie's election by putting his 147 pounds of ruggedness squarely behind him. Returning to Pittsburgh, he was presented with a tuxedo, made a, member of the Dapper Dens, and feted as only Pittsburgh knows how to fete its heroes. Three days later he went to the gymnasium for his first work-out since winning the title and one newspaper noted that he arrived in the tuxedo, reluctant to exchange it for boxing trunks. Presently he was back in the Garden with Armstrong.

Without equivocation, he promised "I'll knock him out in the twelfth." And he knocked him out in the twelfth. Over the radio, his words choppy and fast, he said "Hello, all my friends in Pittsburgh." Then he singled out his brother Pete, proprietor of a, saloon in Lawrenceville. "Hey, Pete, give everybody in the house a drink on me."

Pete phoned local newspapers the next day.

"Fritzie," he said with brotherly annoyance, "ain't paid for all them drinks he told me to give the customers the night he won Armstrong's title. Put that in the paper and oblige."

With the Zivics, Cuddy DeMarco is on friendly terms, but of the five he knows Jack best. Twice they fought and twice he whipped Jack.

"So-o-o," Cuddy said as we pulled out of Garfield, "let's trundle over to Saint Peter's saloon in Lawrenceville. The Zivics knew Greb, and so did most of their customers."

For years, through Harry Keck's breezy Sun-Telegraph column, I kept abreast of doings at Pete's saloon. And via other sources I had got drink-by-drink-sometimes blow-by-blow—descriptions of other doings which, probably because of the paper shortage, escaped the prints.

A sign on the side of the building in Butler Street reads :

Lousy Liquor
Bum Beer
Worse Wine
Filthy Food

Inside, hanging from the top of the bar mirror, another sign reads:

Pete, Oldest and Smallest
But Smartest Zivic
Sports Arguments
Settled

Someone yelled, "There's little Cuddy DeMarco, Greb's old stablemate. Gees, was he hot! Him and Greb was the hottest Pittsburgh ever turn out."

Almost everybody in the saloon had either been in the ring or associated with it. There was a hush as admirers gathered around the once Great Little Man, first one and then another firing questions. Cuddy answered them with grace and finality. Then he inched over to the bar behind which was Pete Zivic. Wearing a sports, jacket more brilliant than an Arizona sunset and nonchalantly twirling his smokeless long-stemmed Dunhill, Cuddy said, "Good evening, Mr. Physic."

"Evenin' Cuddles," said Pete, who with his brother Jack was on the American Olympic boxing team in 1920 and who, with Jack (they were, respectively, a bantamweight and welterweight), went far after turning professional.

Pete's wife, Katherine, twice his size, said in an off-hand way, "How'dy Cuddles. I want to see you before you leave. Want to order some stuff."

Cuddy's right hand swept majestically and instinctively to his chest as, bowing low, he said, "But definitely, old deah."

"Don't forget," Katherine said.

"Righto, my precious dumpling."

An ex-pug sided up.

"Would Billy Conn whip Greb?"

"Charley," Cuddy said, "you know better than ask a question like that. Billy is one of the greatest boxers I ever saw. I think he'll whip Louis next summer. But who can say what he would have done against Greb?" He fumbled for a match, got it, and puffed hard on his pipe. "If you're interested in something about which I can be definite, let me tell you this: Greb was the greatest fighter of his time—greater than Dempsey, Tunney, Mickey Walker—and they were three of our greatest champions."

"A toast to Harry Greb," Pete Zivic said, holding up a glass of beer. "You didn't have to see him fight to know he was a champion. All you had to do was watch him scurry into the ring."

After several drinks the novelty of Cuddy's presence had worn off. An obnoxious little man said, "You didn't whip Tommy Passifume."

Pete Zivic yelled from the end of the bar, "I whipped Passifume."

"So did I," Cuddy said.

"Like hell you did." The obnoxious man moved close, his eyes slits of meanness. He put his guard half-way up, but wisely reconsidered. Cuddy just stood there, smiling and. puffing on his pipe. He didn't even bother to remove his tortoise-rimmed glasses, much less put his hands up, but he was in position to duck a blow and to counter with one of his own.

"Who is the ill-mannered man?" I asked.

"Never got out of the amateurs," Cuddy said.

Cuddy mosied over to the bar and motioned for Pete to come closer. Pete had a tray of beer on his arm. He put it down and leaned over.

"I understand," Cuddy said as confidentially as if imparting the atomic bomb secret, "that you are a man of little sexual consequence."

"Ditto to you, and also likewise." Pete laughed, pleased with his snappy rejoiner. He looked down the bar, "Jack's down there, see him?"

Jack Zivic was one of the hardest hitters in the ring. He looked no more than three or four years older than the night he flabbergasted pugilism by knocking out Lew Tendler twenty years ago.

"I feel swell," he said, "but my voice has gone back on me. It was all right until a few years ago. Now if I talk more than five minutes it fades to a whisper." It happens to many boxers, usually some years after retirement. It takes a, long time for those punches to catch up with you, but when they do they come with startling suddenness.

Jack grew up practically around the corner from Greb's home and saw him in most of his big fights. "Toughest, smartest and most durable fighter I ever saw," he whispered. "You hear people saying Joe Louis would have whipped him. Well, I'll wager Fritzie's last dollar he wouldn't even have come close. Nobody ever fought that windmill without taking a hell of a pasting."

Fritzie, last of the Zivics in the ring, was fighting Cowboy Reuben Shanks at the Pirates' ball park the next night. Greb had fought there innumerable times, and so had Cuddy, Jack and Pete. Cuddy took Katherine's order—a mop, window screens, bathroom accessories, etc. —and we left.

In the cab en route to the ball park the next evening Chris Dundee, Shanks' manager, said he hoped Fritzie would keep his thumbs out of Shanks' eyes. "He's mighty careless with his thumbs," Dundee said. "I always get a fair shake in Pittsburgh, but Fritzie's a pet here and the referee's likely to get fits of blindness."

The day before, Fritzie, who talks faster than Tallulah Bankhead, had disorganised Harry Keck's sports department as he bounced from desk to desk demonstrating punches on members of the overworked staff. He told about his first fight with Shanks. "It was in Minneapolis," he said. "One of Shanks' men came into my dressing room and said, 'Take it easy with the Cowboy tonight, Fritzie. Go ahead and beat him if you can, but don't dissect him. He's only a baby.' "

Fritzie smacked his lips. "Only a baby! But what a tough baby! I went into the ring with the wrong attitude and he out-galloped me. I'll fix him tomorrow night, wait and see."

Out at Forbes Field the next evening, sitting at ringside with Cuddy, it seemed almost disrespectful. Greb had turned in some of his most brilliant fights there in an atmosphere so tense that fans were brawling all around the arena, with the customarily nonplussed reporters, handlers and park flunkies yelling like wild men. Now, nearly thirty years later, here was Pittsburgh's most exciting fighter since Greb, but the park was half empty and there were no brawls and little fuss. When Greb was up there under those lights he was in complete command of everyone's attention. By contrast, here was the most colourful fighter in the ring today and the fans, for all the emotion they showed, might as well have been watching a, sparrow fight.

Cuddy and Harry Keck and most of the other ringside experts thought Fritzie had won, but Shanks got the decision. Back in the huge dressing room shared by both fighters, Shanks was pacing back and forth and trying to rub the swelling out of his cheek bone. Monk Ketchel, Fritzie's pal, was storming about the decision and threatening to punch anyone who disagreed with him. Looking at Shanks from across the room, he said, "All you have to do to win in Pittsburgh is to be from out of town." Shanks glanced over, but said nothing. Fritzie, who accepts defeat as gracefully as he does victory, wasn't saying anything. He knew he had won, and he expected a victor's reward, but it hadn't come out that way and he didn't give a damn. Art Hardy, a local Negro boxer, had been stopped by a low blow in a preliminary that followed the main bout. Naked on a rubbing table, he was in terrible pain. Bill Joos, who used to work in Greb's corner and currently is Billy Conn's Pittsburgh trainer, stood around with a forlorn look on his face. He must have been thinking my and Cuddy's thoughts: "If Harry had been out there tonight there would be so God-damned much excitement in here it would take a hundred cops to keep the boys from getting out of hand."

Cuddy and I walked out with Fritzie.

"Greb boxed Tunney three times, didn't he?" Fritzie said.

"Five," Cuddy said. "Five murderous fights, with neither asking quarter, no holds barred."

"I was just a little shaver when Greb died," Fritzie said. "I saw him once, but I was too young to remember what he looked like. Everybody says he was terrific. They say it in San Francisco in New Orleans, in Denver, in Chicago, in Milwaukee, in Boston, in New York, in Philadelphia — everywhere I've fought they say Greb was terrific."

"No matter how much they say it," Cuddy said, "it's understatement. He was so terrific that when he lost a fight it was something like that bromide about a man biting a dog. It was news, usually front-page news."

Fritzie drove home in his Cadillac and Cuddy and I stopped in at the nearby Pittsburgh Athletic Association. A party was leaving as we arrived. One of its members was straggling behind. Introducing us, Cuddy told him I was writing a book about Greb.

"I could write a better book about him than any of you newspapermen," the straggler said, weaving uncertainly. "Know somethin'? Three or four hours before he lost his middleweight title to Tiger Flowers in 1926, some of his friends went into his hotel room. The bed was made up, but the mattress was on a slant and jiggling. They yanked it up and what do you think they discovered between it and the springs? It was Greb, and he was pouring it to a girl who was yelling everything but stop, thief."

Chapter IX

Capture of Baltimore

"Greb was curiously sensitive, oddly vain"—Tunney.

He would get mad and stay mad for what seemed aeons. Never mind why, he was mad all over, wearing an ouch face to prove it, and the peacemaker who intervened would be asking for a double portion of the dry freeze treatment. Yet if trouble stalked, he would bypass whatever was responsible for his attitude, retaining, however, his excuse for it and asserting that he fully expected to pick up where he had left off when the emergency no longer existed. Then he would go to your aid with every ounce of his fearless heart.

Bleak, indeed, was the morning of May 24, 1922. One of Greb's oldest friends, a reporter, had showed up for the weigh-ins for the first Tunney fight. Outside the boxing commission offices stood a cluster of other reporters, justifiably disgruntled at being barred from what frequently is the scene of raucous leg-pulling and name-calling not only by opposition handlers but by the fighters themselves. Sometimes it is window-dressing, sometimes not, but its potentialities as a funny-bone massager are unlimited.

"If Greb wasn't in the throes of one of his mads at me," the old friend said, "I would go to him and he would put a stop to this nonsense. But he has been mad for months and I'll be damned if I'm going to submerge my feelings by apologising for being right."

As he started down the stairs Greb came jumping up-three steps at a clip. Noting the gloom with which he was enveloped, Greb made the first overtures and then asked why so much unhappiness reigned on this festive day.

"The boxing commission," the friend said, "has barred reporters from the weigh-ins."

"I'm not speakin' to you," Greb said, half annoyed, half amused, "but they can't do that even to you."

He took him into the commission offices, but an officious boxing official ordered the friend out.

"Okay," Greb said stoutly. "If my pal don't stay I don't get on the scales. I ain't fightin' tonight, neither, see?"

Whether it was an act or not, Tex Rickard didn't know Greb well enough at that early stage of their dealings to be sure. But he wasn't taking any chances with his highly ballyhooed title fight being thrown away because of the self-importance of a minor boxing official.

"Don't do nothin' rash," he drawled. "I'll have that ban lifted right now."

It was done and Greb, beaming his pleasure, hauled off his clothes, threw a towel around his lean loins and zestfully stepped on the scales.

But this mad at his old friend, forgiven when trouble befell him, was nothing compared with the high dudgeon into which he was plunged two years later. Directed at no particular individual but at three quarters of a million of them, it was his native and beloved city of Pittsburgh upon which he concentrated the full force of his wrath.

A conventioneer, or what had every appearance of one inadvertently dropped the remark that broke the camel's back. Standing on the fringe of a crowd in the lobby of the William Penn, he pointed to Greb, who was strolling by.

"The only man," he said, "who has ever whipped Tunney."

"By Jesus!" Greb squealed, "that's the hundredth time I've heard that crack today. People point at me like as if I was a statue. What if I did whip Tunney? Ain't it enough that I'm Harry Greb, the middleweight champ, without no more identification?"

He said he was tired, too, of being a prophet in his own town and had decided to remove to Hollywood, "where," it pleased him to dream, "the pastures are greener and the skirts swishier. I'll fight a coupla ginks out there and then maybe I'll bust into the movies."

A journalistic friend, tried and true, advised him to think it over carefully.

"The competition on the coast," he cautioned, "isn't nearly up to par for the course. The fans'll get tired of watching you massacre their bums, and you'll be looking for work, and the promoters will have it for everybody else but you.` The Greb vanity and pocketbook will suffer. What will be the first thing that pops into your head? Pittsburgh, where everybody loves you. And what will you do? Come home with your tail between your legs and that hang-dog look. And the reaction? Your former admirers will say,'Haw! Notice what the flood washed up !' "

"Would you call Jack Reeves a bum?" Greb asked, taking exception to the slur on the Pacific coast's ring talent.

"I don't know," the journalist hedged, "but I doubt that he's any ball of fire."

"That ain't half the things you don't know but have plenty of doubts about."

"What I said still holds. The first time you butt, kick, gouge and bite a native son into oblivion the fans'll put you on their backhouse list and promoters won't dare show you anymore."

"Pretty clever thinkin'," Greb said grumpily, "but it don't apply to me. Maybe I'll have my nose rebuilt. Then I'll be pretty again, and binge, I'll be emotin' on the screen and a new star will be born."

After putting in a final crushing blast at Pittsburgh, he shook its cinders from his shoes.

The first significant word that trickled back was from Oakland. A news-agency dispatch told how he had been met at the train by a raft of sports writers, most of whom had never before enjoyed the privilege of gazing at his inexhaustible physique. A spokesman said he and his colleagues were looking forward to watching him box tough Jack Reeves, adding, "We'll accompany you to the gym to see you limber up."

"I'm not gonna limber up," Greb said. "Me, I been fightin' steady and I'm already as pliable as a innertube."

"But," the spokesman said, "there's a three-deep block-long line in front of the gym and the fans will think hospitality begins and ends in the West if you don't limber up."

The news-agency item said Greb agreed to work out and on the way to the gymnasium he yawned and stretched like an over-hunted foxhound and bewildered the scribes by asking if perchance any of them knew how many rounds the fight was scheduled for. Told that it was only four, he stared vacuously out of the cab and finally said, as if something was demanded of him, "(I hear Reeves is goin' good, hotter'n a debutante and knockin' the boys cuckoo."

The pastures didn't prove as green as he had thought they would. On the contrary, they turned brown from the scorching of the fans, who yelled skunk, scoundrel, rogue, loafer and so forth after he had used up Reeves so badly his mother mistook him for a totem pole.

It was all Greb needed to make him forget about being a prophet back home, where, unlike those uncomplimentary Californians, the fans merely smiled and collected their bets as his victims, like sick dogs, limped off to lick their wounds. What he craved was Pittsburgh. But to return—and save face—he needed an excuse. A fight in the east would provide it. So he pleaded, via telegraph, with his journalistic friend to put a bee in some promoter's bonnet.

"I'll fight anybody anywhere and for anything," he coaxed. "Just get me back home to them golden streets."

Cunningly, ever so cunningly, this imperishable gentleman of the press suggested to Benny Franklin, Baltimore's Tex Rickard, that it would be less than difficult to secure the ring services of the world's undisputed and most rambunctious middleweight champion.

"Who," Franklin asked, "would I put him in with and how much would Greb work for?"

"Feed him Fay Keiser in a non-title bout," the journalist said authoritatively, "and he'll work for doughnuts."

"But Greb has whipped him something like eleven times," Franklin said, dubious of the match's drawing power.

"Sure—in Connellsville, Lonaconing, Philadelphia, twice in Pittsburgh and Cumberland, and all over the landscape, but never in Baltimore. Why the partiality?"

Keiser was a Maryland product (Lonaconing, I think), tough as a turkey gobbler and a name fighter both in America and Europe. He boxed Soldier Bob Martin for the A. E. F. heavyweight title in France and it was the consensus of everybody except the judges and referee that he had won. Mustered out of the service in 1919, he fought Martin in Baltimore. By some strange coincidence the ring lights went out every time Soldier Bob was in trouble and when they came back on he was all right again. It was under these mystifying circumstances, after being flattened at least once, that Martin won the second fight. Jimmy Bronson was his manager. Bronson had been in charge of A. E. F. boxing and after the war had given Martin the benefit of his versatility. Later Bronson was in charge of Tunney's corner that night of the long count in Chicago. Still later, having been on the wagon seven years, he fell off, played a game of football in his apartment with me after his wife had yanked him home by the ear, and between quarters he expressed with goose-pimple feeling his appreciation for those intellectual lights in Baltimore.

"None but a brilliant engineer," I said, "could have so smartly inspired those lights."

"I never even matriculated at M. I. T.," said Mr. Bronson, which gives you an idea of the latent talent of this self-made mechanical genius.

But the Martin fight established Keiser as a box-office draw. And in there with the terrific Greb he figured to break the turnstiles down. Promoter Franklin saw the light quickly and began thumping the ballyhoo tom-toms—with heartening results—even before communicating with Greb. Then he telegraphed him an offer of three thousand dollars to meet Keiser in a non-title fight.

Greb was so anxious to return east that he skipped the "non-title" angle of the offer as if it were a flabby old doll and to Franklin's astonishment not only accepted the match but volunteered to weigh in at 160 pounds. This could mean but one thing—he was going to defend his title.

Tex Rickard would have paid him three thousand dollars for the privilege of introducing him from the ring in street clothes. It worth more than that just to see him hop through the ropes, bow his busted phiz, then hop out without so much as striking a fighting stance.

The apoplectic Franklin, a former bantamweight boxer who had flowered into 250 pounds of irregular shoreline, couldn't fathom it. While he was still in his reverie, he got out life-size posters of the principals, announcing that their coming encounter was the biggest thing since Lord Baltimore's landing.

Greb's journalistic benefactor was waiting on the station platform when the champ slid off the still moving train a month later. In character with a Greb arrival, a brace of high-stepping ladies slid off behind him. Introducing them as Hollywood glamour girls—though they were something less than that—he said, "They're for you, sweetheart." He stepped back, eagerly expecting an appreciative nod, only to discover that journalists are sometimes peculiar critters.

"No, thanks," this one said. "I don't want to go to the sneezer on the Mann Act."

Neither did Greb, when the possibility occurred to him. It was no time to get entangled in the mathematics of the girls' immediate future. So, smiling like a bashful country bumpkin, he said, "It's been nice knowin' you. Gimme a ring some time." And he left them, looking very forlorn, on the station platform.

The journalist looked him over and what he saw did not impress him.

"You don't look much like a movie star," he said, recalling Greb's broadcast threat to join ranks with the celluloid colony.

Greb ignored the sally. He was obligated and he was not unmindful.

On the way to the hotel the journalist said, "You damn fool, why did you sign for a title defence when Franklin offered to show you at over-the-weight, with no risk involved even if you fell down and broke your pendulum?"

"I didn't sign to defend no title," Greb said soberly.

"Actually," the journalist said, "you didn't. You didn't sign a contract in the presence of the proper legal authorities, but you signed your name to a telegram in which you volunteered to make 160 pounds. Franklin assumed, as anyone else would, that you expected Keiser to make the same weight. Since that's the middleweight title poundage, it automatically calls for a championship fight and it has been billed as such."

"Anyhow," Greb said, dismissing the matter in the same suave manner in which he would sneak over a punch on the breakaways, "I ain't defendin' my title and takin'" a chance of losin' it on a hometown decision, or a foul, or somethin'—not for a measly three thousand potatoes."

Momentarily stunned by the inartistic shelving of a deal for which Greb alone was responsible, the journalist pulled himself together with difficulty. "Do you know the date of the fight?" he asked.

"Some night this week."

"Tomorrow night. You barely got in under the wire. Franklin was having hot and cold flashes-."

"He's the right age," Greb broke in, "but I swear I didn't know he was put together like that."

"Never mind the tin-canning. Not hearing from you after accepting the bout, he was getting ready to call it off and leave town ahead of the rotten eggs. And I was ready to follow him."

"I never run out on a fight yet," Greb grumbled. "Me, I'm reliable."

'If you don't defend your title tomorrow night the boxing commission may question your reliability."

Greb's jowls were beefy. He was woefully out of condition.

"Been training hard?" the journalist asked sourly.

"Between us, no. I ain't had a glove on since the Reeves fight a month ago in 'Frisco. But why should I worry? I've beat Keiser eleven times. Eleven out of eleven is pretty fair shootin', ain't it'"

"Then," the journalist rasped, "what are you worrying about tomorrow night for?"

Greb realized he had led with a sucker punch and refused to answer. When he came out of his shell he suggested he talk with the chairman of the boxing commission and Franklin.

"Let's get going," the journalist said, trying to stave off an awful case of the jitters.

Between long periods of small talk Greb asked for every imaginable concession but refused to grant a single one himself. The boxing commissioner sought to break the monotony.

"Harry," he said, putting their discussion on a more personalized basis, "how much do you weigh?"

"Hundred seventy-three and a half."

"Hmf! A little bulky for a middleweight champion defending his title. In fact, the way I count it, thirteen and a half pounds too bulky."

Greb squirmed

"'What's Keiser weigh?'"

"Hundred eighty," the commissioner lied. He was joshing Greb, knowing that Keiser had peeled down to 158+

Greb had been reclining on the bed. He jumped up.

"Sonofabitch!" he yelled.

"What does that make you?" the commissioner taunted.

Greb sat down on the bed and didn't say anything. It was three o'clock in the morning, with the fight less than twenty-four hour away, and all parties were fighting off sleep.

Finally, having asked for everything but conceding nothing, Greb tumbled over and went to sleep.

Came nine o'clock that evening. Greb sauntered into his dressing room, his hat pulled down to hide the scars over his blind right eye. With him, among others, was Al Foss, a referee he had picked up between trains the day before in Pittsburgh.

"The best referee in the world," he said, by way of subtly announcing that his own private referee would be the third man in the ring.

The commissioner saw through the thin veil.

"Charley Short," he said, "is going to handle the fight. He's the best referee in Baltimore and that's good enough for us."

Greb said no.

The commissioner said yes.

He harangued Greb, who said no, no, no with stubborn and increasing emphasis. Exasperated, the commissioner whooped, "What's your objection to Short?"

"I'm afraid he'll let Keiser claim my title on a foul. Fay is pretty cute, you know. He don't think nothin' of foulin' you and he squawks when you foul him back. He may go down holdin' his balls and screamin' 'foul' and Short'll give him my title."

The commissioner paled, his breath whistled through drawn lips and his shoulders slumped. "Is that all that's worrying you?"

"Sure."

The commissioner turned to Short, who meantime had popped into the dressing room.

"Charley," he said, "if Keiser goes down count him out. No matter if Greb's handlers jump into the ring and fell him with an ax and Greb jumps up and down on his chest, count him out."

"Okay;" Short said. "I'll count him out irregardless of how he hits the deck or what keeps him down there."

"Does that suit you, Harry?" the commissioner said.

"No. I still don't trust Short."

"Okay," the commissioner groaned. Glancing nervously at Franklin, he said, "Benny, have the announcer inform the customers that the world's middleweight championship has been called off. Tell them to stop at the ticket window, where their money will be refunded. You'll have to pay the preliminary boys, and you'll lose a wad of money, but it'll come back to you."

Wheeling around, he looked Greb in the eyes. There was just one logical reason why he didn't sock him on that big, scrambled nose: Greb would have socked him back.

"I'll bar you from boxing in Maryland and everywhere I can extend the ban," the commissioner shouted. "Benny will refund the money to the customers and you will have a lawsuit on your hands."

The commissioner moved toward the door. Franklin followed.

"Hey!" Greb yelled in the routine manner in which, five minutes after introduction, he would ask a girl to pull up her skirts, "not so fast. Can't we compromise?"

"What the hell," the commissioner wailed, "do you think I've been trying to do ever since you hit town?"

Greb then suggested that roly-poly Franklin, whose blood pressure was so high it had broken most of Johns Hopkins' shygmomapnometers, be permitted to referee to save his own show. It was against the rules for a promoter to have any connection with a fight beyond promoting it, but in a situation like this strict adherence to ethics can cause a man to famish. Franklin finally consented and the commissioner grudgingly sanctioned it. There was still the matter of Greb's excess weight, since he was 131½ pounds over the middleweight limit and the customers had paid to see a championship fight.

"I won't be too technical about it," the commissioner said.

As Greb hustled up the aisle to the ring wild-eyed spectators grabbed crazily at his blue dressing gown in vain attempts to tear off souvenirs. A hero! Their hero!

Saying "Tonight's contest is for the world's middleweight championship, fifteen rounds to a decision," the announcer read off the weights: Greb 159, Keiser 158½

The commissioner turned to the journalist.

"Fastest piece of shrinkage I ever saw. Ten minutes ago that bastard weighed 173½. If I had a hot poker, one guess what I'd do with it—if I had somebody to hold him!"

Promoter-Referee Franklin instructed the fighters, then told them to come out fighting at the bell. He followed Greb to his corner.

"Get it over with quick, Champ," he whispered. "I'm wore out and can't stand no more excitement."

"Send that tiger over here," Greb spat, "and I'll turn him into an ashcan."

The bell rang for Round One.

Greb stood in his corner and waited for Keiser to come across the ring to meet him. They clashed—in the twelfth and last of their series of roughhousers but the first to which Baltimore had exposed-with Greb's right hand clutching the top rope. With his left extended at full length and his chin tucked solidly behind his uptilted shoulder, he craftily contrived to carve his initials and other fancy designs on Keiser's face and forehead, overlooking nothing in-between. When blood oozed from old cuts, he smeared his gloves in it and dabbed it all around with the dexterity of a watercolour artist. He was intent, his expression serious, for prizefighting was a mean business. He wasn't moving around, just standing there holding onto the rope with his right hand and painting away with his deft left.

He wasn't in shape and was stalling. Rolls of fat bulged over his green trunks. He was puffing like an overloaded railroad engine with its wheels spinning. It was a sloppy, gooey fight, the goo issuing from Keiser. That was all Greb could do to Keiser, who couldn't do anything at all to Greb. The fans responded with mixed cheers, catcalls, foot-stompings, hisses and boos, but mostly boos, and these were for the man who had heard them in all those other places and didn't like them—not even in the mellow city of Bal'more.

Came, after much puffing and fumbling, the twelfth round. Keiser closed in and Greb thumbed him in the left eye. Touche! The champ was beginning to look good as his suet melted away and the speed returned to his powerful legs.

Keiser held his left hand over his eye and, head in butting position, dived in. Greb was hot now, hot as a debutante. He raked his knees over Keiser's groin in a clinch, bringing his hands down to that region where an accurate jolt can make you doubt there is a Santa Claus. With no obstruction to deter him on the road to Keiser's eyes, Greb gave them a liberal treatment with his thumbs.

Keiser jumped back, groaning, and protested to the referee. Franklin inspected his eyes. Finding them still in their sockets, he slapped Greb on the back, signifying that everything was rosy. Greb leaped high into the air and flung an angular left hook. It caught Keiser off balance and dropped him.

It was just the moment Franklin, ready to drop from exhaustion, had been looking for. He straddled Keiser's legs as he started to rise.

"Nine, ten," he yelled without starting at one and counting up to eight. Probably the fastest count in pugilistic history, it was a knock out for Greb.

Unhurt, Keiser scrambled up as his belligerent handlers swarmed into the ring. Greb's men swarmed in, too, but he ushered them out before hell could break loose. Looping his left arm around Franklin's beefy superstructure, he scampered across the ring with it. The limp but meticulous arbiter looked back.

"Winner, and still champion—Greb!" he shouted, making it official.

Bearing a water bucket, water and medicine bottles and sections of a broken stool, Keiser's men took after them. But the fleet Greb, still holding onto his weary quarry, galloped off to safety.

There was not the remotest resemblance to a high pontifical mass in Greb's dressing room, what with the Keiser contingent bellowing defiance and trying to knock the door down from the outside, and the boxing commissioner on the inside demanding an explanation for Franklin's unprecedented actions. (Why, oh, why didn't Mr. Mencken, a Baltimorean and the world's most colourful wordsmith, recapture this intolerance and set it down for future generations in Supplement One, *The American Language?*)

Greb kept a hand on Franklin's pulse until it had idled down to 150. "It's safe to talk now, Benny," he said.

His voice thin and uneven, Franklin's explanation was masterful in its simplicity.

"If I hadn't 'a' took steps to end it when I did," he said, "I'd 'a' collapsed from exhaustion. I was plumb wore out." He wobbled off to a Turkish bath to try to forget. Dead these many years, his friends say he might still have been around if it hadn't been for the Greb fight.

Greb put his clothes on and went outside. Two thugs motioned him and a handler into a cab and drove to the outskirts of town, where they opened the door and, hands moving suggestively in bulging pockets, said "Git and don't come back."

Greb glanced at his trembling handler.

"Can you beat it?" he said; "I inconvenience myself to come here to fight their boy, and I beat him, and now they toss me out o' town. I never seen such ingratitude."

If he inconvenienced himself by going to Baltimore, he also inconvenienced a lot of hotel guests as he was leaving for the arena. It was unintentional, of course, but there was this situation:

His retinue got out of the elevator on the ground floor, but he didn't. With Greb the only passenger, the elevator stopped between the top floor and roof for several minutes.

What was the idea?

"The girl operator," said one of his party, "had fixed him with an inescapable eye. So when we got out, she slammed the door before anyone else could get in and up she went with Greb, staying there until completion of a satisfactory merging of mutual interests. We was all happy, if guests waiting for the elevator wasn't, because it was the kind of roadwork that always sharpened his timing."

Chapter X

Sign-Language Linguist

No fighter was more brilliant than Greb when he was having a good night—and mostly he had good nights. He was not a standup, wasteless-motion stylist like Louis but a lunging, loose-limbed jumping jack, a human windmill that never ran down. He held his hands low and close to his body, sometimes dangling at his sides. He looked as easy to hit as the side of a mountain, but was elusive as a shadow, a deceptive slugger who ran in on punches and smothered them, or pulled away from them before they snapped on him, thus destroying their rhythm and, naturally, effectiveness.

He was not, in the strict sense of the term, an in-and-outer. But when he wasn't brilliant he was awful. Slow and out of skew, a perfect target for any kind of punch—even a sucker punch a novice could avoid—he couldn't untrack himself. Though he fought back aggressively and savagely, a lambasting humiliated him the way a slap humiliates a sensitive child. In the clinches, he would glance at pals in ringside seats and his proud eyes said, "Jesus, ain't it disgraceful? But I'll take care of the next guy the next time out." No one envied his next opponent.

There was no better judge of another fighter than Greb after he had fought him. Following the announcement of the first Dempsey-Tunney match in 1926, when everybody-experts included—was saying Tunney wouldn't last two rounds, Greb was saying the reverse with emphasis.

"I fought 'em both," he said (Dempsey only in the gymnasium but for the kill). "Gene's too smart for him. He'll counter-punch him silly. He's tough as hell, too, and the best body puncher I ever fought. He looks like a gentleman in the ring, and he acts like one, but there the resemblance will end if Dempsey plays rough."

He fastened a militant eye on a reporter who some time before, writing about one of his fights, had rather strongly insinuated there was room for doubt as to whether Greb's ring tactics were pure as the driven snow.

"But you guys don't know nothin' about fightin', and you'll mislead the public, and a lotta suckers which are as big dopes as you are will lose their dough bettin' on Dempsey." (Dempsey entered the ring a three and four-to-one favourite that September evening at the close of Philadelphia's Sesquicentennial. In a downpour that started with the opening and continued through the tenth and final round, decommissioning telegraph instruments and reporters' typewriters, the biggest crowd `ever to witness a prizefight—120,757—blinked in bewilderment as he floundered awkwardly all over the slippery ring. Dempsey was no match for Tunney, and Greb was there to see his prediction come true and to help friends lug away their winnings.)

While one of Greb's attributes was not always tactfulness, it was out of the ordinary for him to talk so harshly unless he was building up to something. In this case, though some schools of diplomacy would probably advise a different approach, he was leading up to a plug for a fighter in whom, quite secretively, he was financially interested. He said this man, a deaf mute, combined the qualities of a ferocious lion and the skill of a champion fencer. How then could Greb better serve a deserving public than by permitting the reporter to present these facts to his thirsty readers? Not a word got into the paper, proving that umbrage still rides the journalistic range. It proved even more-i.e., that this journalist had a long memory, particularly for Greb's recommendations of fighters he had never fought, and he hadn't fought the mute. Vividly he remembered Tex Rickard excitedly shifting from foot to foot as Greb lavished praise on a fighter from Arizona. "Didja fight him, Harry?" Rickard asked.

"No, but I seen him fight and I'm tellin' you, Tex, there's nothin' in the East which can stand up to him."

Sold, Rickard brought Greb's choice all the way from Phoenix to Madison Square Garden and put him in the semifinal to one of Greb's title fights. After that, when Greb recommended a fighter, Rickard always asked, "Didja fight him, Harry?" If Greb said no, Rickard changed the subject.

As Greb saw it, it was up to him to prove that while he sometimes hadn't called the turn on fighters he hadn't fought, he wasn't always wrong. He would go ahead with his original plan, which was to unveil the mute in a small mining town, and the reporter would be sorry he hadn't come through with a plug when a few days later the nation's headlines heralded the new ring sensation.

Gathering up the reliable Happy Albacker, who would have preferred the comparative safety of being shot out of a cannon as opposed to driving with him, Greb took off for the scene of the unveiling. Pitting their talents as seconds against those of the opposition, they expected to boot home a winner.

Until Mr. Albacker's voice became an unintelligible rasp, he gave primitive expression to his displeasure at the speed with which they were plunging over devilish mountain roads and sliding around turns. Greb drove as he fought and that wasn't always pretty.

"I can't stand it no longer," Mr. Albacker gasped. "Stop this coffee grinder and leave me out."

"Whatcha wettin' your pants about?" Greb jerked. "I ain't killed nobody yet."

Mr. Albacker was not one to strive for originality when his future was so uncertain.

"There's always a first time," he gulped.

"This ain't it. Take a swig out'n that bottle and leave the drivin' to me."

No short-change artist in the jug department, Mr. Albacker swigged himself into a comfortable state of anaesthesia.

"I woke up," he said, still trembling after twenty years of trying to forget, "a hundred yards this side of the Rock of Gibraltar which had slid down off of the hill and stopped in the middle of a u-turn."

On the qui vive and in search of the truth, he asked Greb, noted for his honesty, if there was any possibility of missing the rock.

"No," Greb grunted, keeping his reputation intact.

Pulling Mr. Albacker from under the wreckage, he naively asked, "Are you hurt, Hap?" You're okay ain'tcha?"

"If you was hurt you'd know it. I found that out from experience." He wasn't exaggerating. Greb had been in almost as many automobile wrecks as fights. He should have been allergic to both, but he wasn't.

Following a cursory examination and finding that Mr. Albacker was still warm and, if somewhat laboriously, breathing, Greb said, "I ought rattle one off'n your big nose and for two cents I would. Why didn't you tell me that rock was there? You know I can't see ten foot ahead o' me."

Unhappily, Mr. Albacker knew all about Greb's bad eyes, but for which knowledge he wouldn't have felt the necessity of lulling himself into false security via the jug. Nor would he have climbed into Greb's car with such nightmarish fearfulness. It was not, however, the time or place for a learned discussion of careful vs. reckless motoring, or why Greb, who couldn't see the Taj Mahal under a spotlight, didn't turn the wheel over to his pal who could see a gnat's eyes at fifty paces.

"We was only two-three miles from our destination," Mr. Albacker said, "so we walked the rest of the way."

Greb, to whom physical fear was as foreign as originality to a copyreader, couldn't understand why Mr. Albacker was quaking.

"I desired to get my mind off of the shrill sound of steel contacting rock," Mr. Albacker said, "so I started talking about something else."

He asked Greb to tell him more about the deaf mute.

"My dummy's a helluva puncher and slick a boxer as you ever seen," Greb said. "If he don't run into no trouble tonight, which I don't figger he will, he'll be workin' in the Garden for Rickard before you can say scat."

He said the deaf mute's affliction, though regrettable, was not without its advantages to his pugilistic board of strategy.

"I don't have to listen to no squawks," he said with the rakishness of a loquacious fight manager detailing for the press his own trials but ignoring those of his meal ticket who, of course, doesn't do anything but catch those wallops to head and body. "All he can do is grunt and make signs. If I don't feel like watchin' while he beefs I can be blind."

In his sometimes disorderly mind, Mr. Albacker usually thought Clearly in situations in which his pal was involved. Currently, there were the answers to these questions that interested him; did the mute merit the match, or did the promoter give it to him off Greb's drawing power as a second? How was Greb going to talk to his property? Did he know the sign language?

Reluctantly, and with much grumpiness at being pinned down, Greb supplied the replies: "It was my drawing power that got the match. Sure I know the sign language. I took a couple o' lessons and I'm practically a sign-language linguist."

He then dropped some unsolicited but nonetheless revealing information. Out of friendship (for Greb), the referee and one of the judges were going to see everything the deaf mute did to his opponent but nothing that was done back to him. In some of the smoother circles along Jacobs Beach, that strip of sidewalk in West Forty-ninth Street between Broadway and Eighth Avenue in the shadow of Madison Square Garden, this is known as-fits Of blindness. Peculiar to certain boxing officials, it manifests itself following brotherly love overtures in which something of substance is dropped into the conveniently upturned palm of the afflicted. Not yet isolated by medical researchers, it narrows the vision of its victims to one object. Across the years it has provoked so much pent-up feeling that hordes of collaborators have deemed it wise to hasten from the scene of action in order to avoid ugly situations. In fact, though innocent as a dove, I was once clocked burning up a hundred yards in ten seconds while pacing a group of collaborantionists on whose side God didn't seem to be one evening when their boy got the decision after being rendered null and void twice in the last round.

No matter where Greb went or what he did there was excitement. He attracted it merely by being in the neighbourhood. And this night in the mining town was no exception. The main bout, in which his mute was to participate, was in the ring but was being held up pending his arrival. Half of the customers, thinking they had been lured into the arena by a promoter who had no intention of producing Greb as a second, were stampeding the ticket window, demanding refunds. The other half was booing while the glib announcer told one pointless joke after another In an effort to quiet them.

Now the fight fan who thinks he has been fleeced and rises to give physical force to his thoughts is as awkward to handle as a horned toad. It takes an adept and fearless psychologist to bring back to his distrusting heart the urge to love thy neighbour. There is no time to debate whether to resort to Routine X2 or drop the matter and get the hell out of there. Greb had been in dark places before. He had been in yawning canyons where the only light was Satan's flash. He knew one command, one impulse, and that was attack.

Arriving half an hour late, he elbowed through the angry crowd, parting it as a cutter parts water. Few fans had ever seen him in street clothes, but he was no less impressive. Jumping into the ring, his eyes a challenge, his powerful body rippling defiantly, his indictment of the customers as thieves and crums was so individualised that it had them looking accusingly at one another. It quieted malcontents and the fight got under way immediately.

In rapid succession the mute went down three times. He didn't know how to box his southpaw opponent. He kept looking to his corner for instructions. Greb would give them frantically with his hands, the mute would follow them and ping, he was sitting on his haunches. Scrambling up, he would glance at his corner, get the signal and follow instructions. His usual reward was an uncomfortable visit to the floor. Presently, he would shake his head no and grunt. Greb would shake his head yes, gesturing crazily with his hands. The mute would do as he was told and with the same discouraging results. His only consolation was that he couldn't hear the vile names Greb was shouting at him.

Back in his corner it was the same thing—the mute grunting and shaking his head no, Greb yelling and nodding yes and re-emphasising the signal. Protestingly, the mute would execute orders, step into a swinging left and plummet to the floor.

Before the bell rang for the eighth and final round the referee went over to the mute's corner.

"Harry," he said to Greb, "I can't give this fight to your bum. He's been down ten times already and lost every round."

"Whaddya mean he's lost every round?" Greb said sharply. "He's winning from here to China. He wins on aggressiveness if nothing else. You saw how he waded in there...."

"Yes," interjected the referee, "and lands on his fat ass. He ain't even a amateur."

"If you don't give him the fight you oughta be run out o' town."

"Maybe you would wish," said the referee graciously, "to report us to the boxing commission."

"I wouldn't go no deeper into this discussion," said Mr. Albacker, taking his life in his hands. "The referee's right. The mute woulda did better if he had led with his rump which, judging from the way he lands on it, is less vulnerable than his frontal exposure."

Greb didn't say anything, but the look he gave Mr. Albacker was replete with sabotage.

The warning buzzer rang. As Greb jumped out of the ring he gave final and vigorous instructions with both hands. "What did that mean" Mr. Albacker asked.

"I told him that if he didn't win by a knockout it looks like he'll lose the fight."

"Ain'tcha afraid the information will shock him," said Mr. Albacker wryly, "considering that he's been knocked down only ten times?"

Ignoring Mr. Albacker's humorous spree, Greb said, "Look at that dirty crook (the referee) over there buzzin' the judges. He's tellin' them to vote against my dummy, I bet'cha."

"If you was knocked down ten times in seven rounds, would you consider you had won?"

Greb said this was an irrelevant question and didn't rate a reply. His mute wasn't knocked down anymore, but it was the only round in which he hadn't been down at least once. All three officials voted against him despite the fits of blindness with which two of them had agreed to be enveloped.

On the train some hours later Greb was slouched down in his day-coach seat. Half asleep, he was facing his mute whose head was bandaged up like an Egyptian mummy and whose squeals and motions with his hands were attracting everybody in the car. A passenger came over from a nearby seat.

"You're Harry Greb, aren't you?"

Greb opened his eyes slowly and just as slowly acknowledged his identity.

"I know the sign language," the passenger said. "I saw the fight this evening. Do you know what the mute is making so much fuss about?"

"He's crazy," Greb said, "crazy as a bedbug full o' tobacco juice."

"He's been saying all night that you made him fight his southpaw opponent with a left hand. You meant to give him the opposite signal, but throughout the fight you insisted he use his left and he damn nearly got killed. Giving the signal for the left hand is the easiest sign in finger talking, but I see it was too much involved for you."

The mute sensed what was being said. He tapped the passenger on the back, squealed and made signs that authenticated the explanation.

Greb straightened in his seat. He looked at the grotesquely mutilated and bandaged face of his fighter who was jumping up and down, gesticulating furiously with his hands and squealing like a stuck pig.

For a minute Greb was in a trance. Then half standing, half sitting, he threw his head over the back of his seat and laughed until he was gasping for breath.

"Awful funny!" said Mr. Albacker sarcastically.

"Funniest thing that ever happened to me," Greb said, launching into another and more sustained laugh.

The mute mumbled, slumped down in his seat, wrapped his arms around his head in a futile gesture and went to sleep.

"He's yours, Hap," Greb said expensively. His love for Mr. Albacker was so great that he would give him anything on earth, even his financial interest in his butchered prizefighter.

"Take him to New York on your next trip," counselled Mr. Albacker, "and turn him over to the Egyptian wing of the Metropolitan Museum of Art."

Chapter XI

Gunboat Gave Greb the Nod

The truism that a fighter is no better than his hands didn't apply to two of our greatest fighters —Tunney and Greb. But their methods of overcoming weak hands differed as greatly as their personalities. Tunney kept solid rubber balls in his coat pockets and squeezed them with all his strength when he wasn't otherwise occupied. Finally he moved on to a logging camp in the north country and chopped wood until his once brittle hands were a match for his hitting power.

Greb's was a more primitive, but for him a quicker and just as effective method. Showing up at a hospital with a Colle's fracture of his left hand one day, he impatiently asked to know how long it would keep him out of action.

"At least three weeks," the doctor said.

"Like hell it will," Greb said stubbornly, "I've got a fight coming up this week and no busted hand's gonna knock me out of it."

Then he hopped over to Philadelphia, took the splint off his recently broken and still swollen hand, and when he got through lathering Sailor Petrosky, twenty pounds heavier, tough and ringwise, the Sailor limped off to drydock.

Early in his career Greb had convinced himself that the way to keep in fighting trim was to keep fighting.

"There's no easy way out," he said. "If you lay around your hinges get rusty. If you try to keep in shape working with a paid sparring partner he's liable to hurt you more than an opponent you get paid to fight."

What he advised others to do he did himself. Keeping gymnasium workouts to a minimum, he fought as often as his physique would take it. He was as mindful of the importance of a title defence as any other champion except that he fought on the very eve of it, whereas contemporaries, fearful of injuries that might cause postponements, shuddered at the thought of so much as sparring with their great aunts.

This had been his system from the day he started fighting. It had always been right for him. But as he came down the home stretch in the closing days of his amazing career the strain was evident. In less than a seven-week period he had fought six times, engaged in two unrecorded exhibitions that were rougher than most grudge fights, made a round trip to California, and was in the ring, his middleweight championship the prize, against Tiger Flowers.

He was drawn and tired that February night in 1926, but he was happy. Baltimore admirers had forgiven him for his sloppy performance a year before With Fay Keiser and, converging on his hotel suite, presented him With an expensive navy blue dressing gown.

Then as now no one knew definitely who would referee a fight until the contestants entered the ring. As Greb came into his corner he said to a handler, "Am I seein' things? Is that Gunboat Smith over there?"

It was Gunboat Smith for sure, once a paralysing punching heavyweight and, after his fighting days, a great referee, When he motioned the fighters to the centre of the ring for instructions, Greb trotted over.

"Hello Gunboat, ol' pal," he said, chipper as a robin after a spring rain.

"Where d'ya git that ol' pal stuff?" Gunboat's voice was no friendlier than his words. Six years earlier a careless thumb had dropped into his eye and an almost simultaneous jolt on the chin had knocked him out in Round One.

"Gee," Greb said when he returned to his corner, "I wish I hadn'ta Stuck my thumb in the Gunboat's eye that time in South Bend."

In the other corner Squawk (christened Walk) Miller was instilling confidence in his black campaigner, who was on the short end of five-to-one betting. New York gamblers hadn't forgotten how Greb had enfeebled Mickey Walker only a few months before. They hadn't forgotten, either, how right after that brawl Jack Delaney duplicated the dramatic Kid Norfolk's easy feats by twice flattening Flowers, and how Squawk Miller refused to be convinced there weren't horseshoes in Delaney's gloves. Four other opponents had spiked Flowers to the canvas once apiece. There wasn't much excuse for sending him against the redoubtable Greb except that Flowers had caught him on an off night a couple of years before and held him to fairly even terms in a non-title fight in Fremont, Ohio.

But Tex Rickard usually had a reason up his long sleeve. Greb was a money maker. The fans followed him whether they loved him or hated him. They knew he wouldn't fumble or posture when the gong rang, and twenty thousand of them, the second largest crowd to file into the new Garden up to then, were on hand to see him in his debut at the uptown version of Stanford White's famous edifice. It was a typical Greb turnout, his Pittsburgh public backing him with vocal cords, money, fists and blackjacks.

He fought a crowding, bulling fight, but he was slow and his timing was bad. Flowers was as nervous as a butterfly with an itchy tail and he flitted about like one, wrapping his arms around his head as he jerked his jitter-bug frame all over the ring. He was as unorthodox as Greb and on top of this he was a southpaw. It was not a cleverly waged bout, but it was exciting and it was pathetic—pathetic because a washed-up Greb was exerting every ounce of his waning energy to hold off an inferior opponent. It was as though Caruso, his voice a thin whisper of what it once had been, were competing with a bierstube tenor for a singing waiter's job.

Flowers was using a, right hand that was a feeble attempt at a hook but was nothing more than an off-balance sideswipe. But he scored with it. As the bout moved into its final stages his fright disappeared and he got rough. Greb was too contemptuous to rough him back. But when the roughing continued and it was apparent Flowers was challenging his mettle, Greb went close and gave him the works—backhand, elbows, thumbs, head, knees— fast like that. Flowers jumped back and protested to Gunboat Smith, who just looked at him.

When it was all over and he had collected the officials' slips, Joe Humphreys, who had grown up with such ring immortals as Terrible Terry McGovern and Stanley Ketchel, glanced at Greb and shook his head helplessly. Then, announcing the decision—and with it the crowning of a new champion—he halfheartedly held Flowers' hand aloft in the customary gesture. Two judges had voted for Flowers. But Gunboat Smith, who had reasons for not loving Greb, voted for Greb.

It is discouraging enough for an ordinary fighter to lose to another ordinary fighter on a split verdict, but when a champion's title is yielded to a challenger with Flowers' spotty record, it is tragic. There was nothing anyone could do about it, least of all Greb. He was a, champion, anyhow. So, back in his dressing room, he talked like one.

"What the hell! Tex is gonna gimme another fight with Flowers. I'll take a good rest, then I'll come back and beat that jig so bad even the judges will have to admit it."

Five months later, mentally relaxed but sharpened by two tune-up fights, he was back in the Garden with Flowers. It wasn't the tireless Greb of old, but it was a somewhat rejuvenated Greb. Taking the offensive at the opening bell, he relinquished it only when it would have been foolhardy not to. Before he went into the ring he said, "I've got one good fight left in me and I'm gonna whip the Tiger sure as hell. If he dogs it tonight, I'm gonna pull 'em up off the floor and try to knock him out with a haymaker."

The crowd was five thousand short of that which turned out for their first Garden fight, but it was none-the-less rabid. The weights were: Flowers 1591, Greb 159. Squawk Miller was in charge of Flowers' corner, James J. Johnston in charge of Greb's. The bell rang. Greb streaked across the ring and raked Flowers with a two-handed body fire. Uneasy under the viciousness of the attack, Flowers immediately complained to the referee about being fouled, and he complained throughout the fight, but it didn't deter Greb. Twice Flowers went down, partly from slips but mostly from an overwhelming desire to get the hell away from there. Greb was down once, but he was wrestled down in a clinch. In the closing rounds, Flowers actually turned and ran. Two or three times, when Greb caught up with him, he doubled him over the ropes and pounded him dizzy.

When Joe Humphreys announced Flowers as the winner—the two judges, but not the referee, voting for him—the fans stormed the ring, littering it with bottles, hats, paper and everything they could find to throw, in protest. Jim Crowley, the referee, walked over to Greb. "Tough, Harry," he said. "A tough one to lose. It was your fight."

Tunney said, "Harry won by a substantial margin. It was an unjustified decision."

William Muldoon said Greb had won, adding, "but the decision will stand. If we (the New York Athletic Commission) reversed it, the Negro people might think they were being discriminated against."

Before Greb entered the ring he had said that, no matter what the outcome, this was his last fight. Now he was through forever with the profession in which he had realised his boyhood dreams. Boxing had been good to him. It had been tough, hut it had been fun, too—lucrative fun. He had see-sawed up and down the pugilistic ladder, losing sometimes but winning most of the time. He hadn't cared a damn so long as he had always given his best—and he always gave his best.

A great champion, he had wanted to be succeeded by a great champion. But it hadn't turned out that way. Standing there in the Garden ring for the last time as fighter, he smiled pensively at the fans who were protesting the injustice of the decision just handed down, and he cried.

"The Tiger is all right," he sobbed. "I got nothin' against him. But —but he's not a champion. He'll lose my title the first time he defends it against anyone who can fight." (The next time Flowers defended his title—it was less than five months later he lost it to Mickey Walker in Chicago.)

Chapter XII

Make It Inter-resting

One morning last summer I was waked by three firm knocks on the door of my William Penn Hotel room in Pittsburgh. I was fairly foggy, having made the rounds of the glitter palaces with Cuddy DeMarco the previous night, but not too foggy to be impressed with the firmness of those knocks. After first trying to reach the door through the bathroom and then a double-door closet, I got my direction and accomplished my mission.

Outside stood three men. Each said, in perfect unison, "Good morning! You are Mr. Fair, we presume."

At that early hour and with such a foggy brain I wasn't so positive of my identity, but since a name had been advanced I took a chance and accepted it as mine.

"You are writing a book about Harry Greb," they said, their mouths opening and closing as if they were on the same string. "We have some stories which we would like to tell you. But first how much is in it for us?"

"Not a goddam cent."

"Very well," said one of them, the other two being too disconcerted to remember their lines. "We will tell you some and if; you like them, you may feel differently about reimbursing us."

After rattling off a couple, which, incidentally, had been pilfered from an article in Esquire's First Sports Reader * entitled The Iron City Express, he waited a moment for my reaction. Glancing back into the semi-darkness of my room I saw two large bare feet ease over the foot of a twin bed. Landing firmly on the floor, they brought Happy Albacker running to my side.

"Are these ginks tryin' to shake you down?" asked the gentleman who many times had acted as bodyguard for the greatest fighting man this land has ever had.

"We are telling him hitherto unpublished stories about Harry Greb," said the man who was not yet disconcerted, "and here is another one; Greb's name wasn't really Greb. It was Berg and he turned it into Greb by spelling it backwards."

"Why you lyin', thievin' impersonators of fleas," said Mr. Albacker decisively, "you've been readin' some of them misinformed sports writers' stories. Git out o' here before I forgit I'm too intellectual to kill."

The three monotonous men left. But I was to hear from them again. A few minutes later one of them telephoned from the lobby.

"If you use our stories, be sure to mention our names," he said, giving all three names and addresses. "And in any event, be sure to make it an interresting book."

There were a lot of callers that morning last summer, but only one of them had known Greb or had honourable intentions.

"I have not come to tell you any stories about Harry," said Henry Bluestone, "but to tell you Ida Edwards has been up in arms ever since Esquire ran an article of yours three years ago called The Wildest Tiger. (Ida Edwards is one of Greb's three sisters. Closer to him than anyone else in the family, she and her husband Elmer adopted his daughter Dorothy following the boxer's death in 1926.)

"What's she angry about?" I asked.

"She didn't like some of the passages in that article, and neither did I."

"But they're all true, and I can't see that they reflected discredit to her brother, who had as much license as any other artist to display his temperament on odd Fridays."

"She's still huffy," Bluestone said, "and she has Harry's tenacity. But she's one of my oldest and dearest friends, as was Harry, and since my sole interest is in seeing that you get an authentic story of his career, I'll be glad to act as intermediary. She knows about your book and is incensed because you haven't tried to see her."

"I'm more anxious to get her side of the story than she is to give it to me," I said, "and as soon as I come to the place where what she has to say will stand out I want to talk with her."

Four days before Ida Edwards and I got together last winter Henry Bluestone was fatally stricken with a heart attack.

It was snowing when I left the William Penn with Ensign Donald Wilhelm, fresh from two and a half years of action in the South Pacific and hero medals on his chest as evidence. En route to the Edwards home we stopped off at the Royal York apartment of Ralph Richards for some turtle soup made, according to our host, from the most intellectual turtle in Tyler county, West Virginia, and captured by that state's most accomplished turtle feeler, same being a sanguinary character named Uticy Bill, who pokes his hand down a hole and, his hand still intact, pulls out a turtle.

As we were leaving, Mrs. Richards said, "Tell the cabby to take you to 121 Mayflower Street. That's the Edwards home."

It was the Edwards home, all right, but not J. Elmer Edwards, husband of Ida, Greb Edwards. By the time we made this discovery our cab was out of sight. It was Sunday night and the snow and wind, as if we were contesting their authority, were lashing us into hitherto unsurpassed unhappiness. The soup from that intellectual turtle, plus the strong water poured by our host, did nothing but impede progress as we skidded backwards going uphill and aimed at trees sliding downhill. We were an hour overdue when we arrived at 6444 Jackson Street, where Mrs. Richards should have sent us in the first place, and we were snowmen with florid complexions. More strong water was essential and Ida, Edwards, looking very young for the mother of two grown daughters (Audrey, her own, and Dorothy Greb Edwards Wohlfarth by adoption) was not slow on the draw.

"Poor Henry (Bluestone) was too young to go," I said. "He had wanted to bring us together in an effort to eliminate any possible friction."

"A very wonderful friend," Ida said. "We used to loaf by the hour at his place." (Spalding's Drug Store.)

She didn't say anything for a moment. Then very gently she asked,

"What kind of book are you writing about our Harry?" "Somewhat spicy. He was not exactly a celibate, you know."

"I know, and I'm not squeamish about his affairs with girls. But he didn't run around with them during his marriage. I wouldn't want anything to reflect on Dorothy's children. It was only after the death of our Harry's wife that he really attained fame. I should like to see what you have written."

"The type is locked up and I haven't any carbon copies or proofs. You'll probably object to some of the passages, but they have been used, as much as anything else, as vehicles to point up Harry's greatness. No other fighter could do what he did and remain at the top of his profession so long."

There was a large hand-coloured photograph of Greb on the wall of the comfortable home he had built in Pittsburgh's beautiful East Liberty. It accentuated his powerful legs.

"They're what pulled him through those awfully hard fights," Ida said.

A headlight flashed against the window and a car, bulky under clinging snow, stopped at the front entrance.

"There she is," Ida said, "always late."

It was Greb's daughter Dorothy, and her husband, Phillip Wohlfarth, Jr. The only other time I had seen her was twenty years ago. Harry Keck and I had just returned from Madison Square Garden after covering her father's third fight with Tiger Flowers. He had lost—not in our or the referee's but in the judges' eyes. We knew it was his last fight. It was a tough one to lose and we had gone to his Claridge Hotel suite to console him. Dorothy was standing near the elevator when we got off. She didn't know us, but her childish intuition told her we were her father's friends.

"Black man did not whip my Pappa," she said firmly. "My Pappa whipped black man."

"Do you remember, Dorothy?" Ida Edwards said. She had brought Dorothy to New York.

"I vaguely remember being there, but nothing more," Dorothy said.

"I remember the dress you wore," I said. "It was red and it flared at the bottom."

"That cute little red velvet dress," Ida said with a bonbon in her heart. "I had forgotten but now I remember."

A former Pittsburgh model, there is a sweep around Dorothy's eyes that makes her look like her father's twin. Though the mother of two children-Harry Greb Wohlfarth Jr., aged six, and Suzanne, aged four—she has the firm figure of a college freshman and is definitely Hollywood material.

"I barely remember Father," she said.

"You don't remember the time he paddled you at his Manhasset, Long Island, trainine camp?" Ida asked.

"No."

Dorothy was four at the time. Photographers had seen her flitting around the grounds and when they learned her identity they nabbed her and posed her for three hours. Peevish from the ordeal, she refused to go to her father when he tried to show her off to friends.

"She came to me instead," Ida said. "Our Harry paddled her and he had to fight me."

When Greb was ten years old he had mapped the course of his future.

"In fact," Ida said, her eyes warm with sisterly love, her voice soft and cultured, "he had already put himself on a pinnacle. He would scurry down into Father's basement, stand on a box, strike a fighting stance and proclaim himself the world's champion."

At the age of ten he didn't bother to designate which one of the eight recognised weight divisions of which he was world's champion. He simply proclaimed himself the world's champion.

Gene Tunney, who of the name fighters fought him more than anyone else, would find no fault with Greb's all-encompassing designation.

"In my eyes," he said, "Harry was the world's champion,"

Greb was a pigeon fancier and he kept a cote on the roof of his father's home.

"He ran away when he was fourteen," Ida said, refuting the familiar story that his father had asked him to leave after Greb had returned home one night and admitted having engaged in a ring encounter. "Eight months later i got word to him that Father was going to sell the pigeons. He hurried home and persuaded Father not to sell - and usually when Father came to a decision it was final. He stayed home six or eight months and then he left again."

Occasionally Greb wrote Ida from Philadelphia, but said little about himself. He didn't tell her that he was fighting such renowned boxers as Mike Gibbons and, though still a kid, whipping them.

"He told me later," she said, "he had been so badly injured in a bout that he was sick for six months. He hadn't any money and he was too proud to tell Father. A baker who was a boxing enthusiast took him into his home and cared for him."

Ida went to Philadelphia with her brother after he had become so famous crowds were following him.

"Our Harry would take no interest in them," she said, "and made a bee-line for the home of the man who had befriended him."

I had heard about the baker. The story was that after Greb had scaled the fistic heights he had showered the old man with gifts and affection. But Ida knew nothing about this phase.

"I don't even remember that wonderful man's name," she said.

The legend of Greb's tremendous stamina, his never-tiring physique no matter how fast or long or punishing the going, is not completely borne out by Ida.

"He would be exhausted following hard fights or long, gruelling preparatory workouts," she said.

Conversely, she remembers so vividly a night in Steubenville, Ohio, a quarter of a century ago. For some unknown reason Greb had been left alone in his dressing room before being called into the ring.

"When Red Mason and Elmer and I returned," she said, "our Harry was lying unconscious on the floor. He had been chloroformed, obviously by gamblers betting against him."

Elmer and Mason held him by the feet while they pushed the rest of him out of a window and swung him to and fro until he was revived. "Still groggy," she said, "he cut to ribbons a man nearly twice his size."

Then there was the night in Pittsburgh when he was boxing Soldier Jones, the Canadian army's hard-hitting heavyweight. Jones kept his right hand cocked against his right shoulder. He was awkward-looking as a trotting cow, but a good hitter and he always gave Greb trouble.

"Our Harry was down six times in two rounds," Ida said. "I sat at ringside and was frantic. It's frightening to see your brother taking all that punishment. The spectators were stunned. You could have heard a pin drop. Welter Monahan, a city patrolman, was kneeling and saying his rosary. Red Mason was so excited he mistook Elmer, who was helping him in the corner, for our Harry and dashed a bucket of water into his face at the end of the second round. (Ed. note—The story I heard was that Elmer needed the water more than Greb did and Mason knew it.)

"Our Harry recovered quickly in his corner and he tore out of it so savagely when the bell started the third that Jones tried to dive through the ropes. Our Harry grabbed him by the loose trunks, yanked him back in and gave him a terrible beating. Sure he had lost, our Harry cried disconsolately after the fight, refusing to believe he had won until early editions of the morning newspapers told of his decisive victory over Jones."

The reliving of that exciting evening out of the past wore Elmer down to a yawning frazzle. It was his bedtime anyway. There had been no casualties. So Ensign Wilhelm and I left with Dorothy and her husband who volunteered to drop us off at the Pittsburgh Playhouse, where Cuddy DeMarco and his wife Ruth were waiting. It was still snowing, the flakes big and fluffy, the temperature mild. It was thrilling sitting there beside the smart daughter of my favourite pugilist.

I said,"Dorothy, you know Cuddy, of course."

"Oh yes. Everybody in Pittsburgh knows Cuddy. I understand he sells everything from diapers to aeroplanes. But every time I see him he says, 'Well, well, Dorothy, I haven't seen you since you were a little tyke.' "

Dorothy said she had seen him fairly recently and that "I haven't been a little tyke for several years."

At the Playhouse the DeMarcos were occupying a table near the entrance.

"Cuddy," I said, "you remember Dorothy Greb Edwards."

"Cer-tain-ly,'" Cuddy said, rising snappily and bowing deeply. "How are you, Dorothy? You were just a little tyke the last time I saw you."

Dorothy said, "It was less than two years ago, Cuddy."

Cuddy said, "Dorothy, my dear girl, it has been longer."

I don't remember the outcome of this friendly discussion, since it continued until Ida's parting hospitable gesture had looped me, spinning me into a non-retentive mental state.

Ensign Wilhelm, player-manager of Stanford University's 1940 football team, had made the trip from New York to see the city so highly publicised by its Pitt Panthers, Fritzie Zivic and Billy Conn.

"You promoted me to Commodore before leaving the Playhouse last night," he said, yawning and stretching his lean frame, "and starting now I wish to be addressed as Commodore."

His eyes fell on a French Renaissance Structure across the street from our room.

"Beautiful," he said. "What building is that?"

"William Penn garage."

"Now come," Commodore Wilhelm said. "That building is as big as the William Penn itself."

"Bigger," I said. "And why shouldn't it be bigger? Because in Order to get a room at the William Penn you have to bring your car and leave it as security. It must be a custom-built Cadillac, complete with housekeeping unit, and if you get it back you're lucky. Ask for Jimmy Greer on the house phone. He'll bear me out."

"You didn't bring a car," Wilhelm said saucily.

"No, but I borrowed one from Sam Mallison, a permanent resident of the hotel, and Greer gave me a room without question."

There was a noise of heavy feet outside our room followed by a bang on the door, which, miraculously, did not cave in under the impact.

"Leave me in."

It couldn't be anyone but Happy Albacker.

"Hap," I said, "isn't that building across the street the William Penn garage?"

"Who says it ain't?"

"An ex-Commodore." I said, demoting Wilhelm that quickly.

After a verbal synopsis of his views on international amity, harnessing of atomic power and the molecular composition of goat milk, Mr. Albacker said he would have to hurry back to the offices of the Allegheny County

Federal Housing Authority, where he is Recreation Director. As he was leaving, Fritizie Zivic shuffled in.

Extending his big paw, Mr. Albacker said, "Thanks, Fritz, for giving that swell talk at the high school for my boys last week. It sure wept over big."

"Glad to do it, Hap. By the way, I'm going to Miami next month (February). Got a fight down there."

"Yeah? Who you fightin'?"

"Damn if I know," said Fritzie, who would have been as little concerned if his opponent had been six Joe Louises rolled into one. "I don't think the promoter told me his name."

"I'm going to Miami, too, Fritz. How's about me refereein' that fight?" Mr. Albacker produced a national referee's license.

"Sure, Hap. You're the best referee in America anyway. I'll tell the promoter I want you to handle the fight. You're as good as in."

They shook hands and Mr. Albacker left, promising to return to the hotel for dinner.

Fritzie threw two pencils on the bed. On their white metallic barrels were his signature and under this his photograph.

"Call me Professor," he said. "I'm a school teacher now. I'm running a boxing school for boys from eight to twelve years old and using these pencils as advertisements. Teaching kids to box doesn't mean they're going to take it up professionally any more than teaching dancing means the pupils will follow it professionally."

Until Webster's comes up with a better definition, unique will have to be the word for Fritzie. It's against boxing commission rules for an active boxer to own boxers. Fritzie owns fifteen. An active boxer is not permitted to Promote bouts. Fritzie not only promotes them but he owns the park (Hickey) in which he promotes during the summer.

There was a bottle of Philadelphia rye on the table. The former world's welterweight champion took a drink, lit a cigarette and threw both legs over the arm of an easy chair.

"I'm so smart," he said in a deprecatory tone, "that I outsmart myself. Last week I sold my Cadillac for twenty-seven hundred. It cost me twenty-five new and it had only thirty thousand miles on it, Then I sold my Chevrolet, taking a good profit. I told Juste Fontaine (the best of Fritzie's stable of fighters) that if he trained hard and won his next bout I would give him a new Ford. He did both. I kept my word; I bought him a Ford from a dealer I know.

"Now what do you think happens? Juste has a, good fight coming up. I move him out to my home in Mount Lebanon so I can watch him. When he goes on the road in the mornings I don't want him to do like I used to do to poor old Luke Carney (Fritzie's deceased manager). I would run until I was out of sight, then sit down and read the funnies and drink a bottle of beer I had squirrelled away under my sweat shirt. Juste isn't going to get away with that kind of stuff with me.

"The first day he hits the road I instinctively go down to my garage and make the startling discovery I haven't a car to my name. When I ask the dealer who sold me the Ford I gave to Juste to send me up another car he laughs and says 'Are you kiddin', Fritz? Ain't you heard about the strike in Detroit?'

"I can't borrow Juste's Ford because he has loaned it to some dame. I can't follow him on the road because I'm too old to stand the pace. I'm in a helluva fix until my kid comes out of the house with his scooter the other day. He squawls for his mother when I grab it away from him. I get on it and take after Juste and pretty soon I catch up with him. Now I'm following him on the kid's scooter."

It was noon and Fritzie had a luncheon

"If you need me," he said, "have me paged at the Roosevelt or here in the William Penn lobby."

On the heels of Fritzie's departure came the ubiquitous Cuddy DeMarco.

"I forgot when I asked you to the house for dinner that Ruth has to have a wisdom tooth pulled today I'm on my way home to take care Of C. O. D. Why not come out after supper? Ruth will be rested by then."

"I've got a date with Dorothy Greb Edwards Wohlfarth around eight tonight Cuddles," I said. "Maybe I can pick you up later if you're still free."

Cuddy wanted to know what New Yorkers are saying about the forthcoming Louis-Conn fight and I said I hadn't heard much comment.

"Billy," he said, "is very great - a very great boxer. He is bigger now than he was for the other Louis fight and he's punching harder. Don't be surprised if he knocks Joe out."

By prearrangement, Ida and J. Elmer Edwards picked up the ex Commodore and me Monday night and carried us, as they say in the Old Dominion, to the Pleasant Hills home of Dorothy and Phillip Wohlfarth, Jr. The snow was thin but slippery and Elmer was afraid to step on the gas at the approach to the last hill. Halfway up his Plymouth whoomped and died.

"I wouldn't want to try walking up this hill without cleats," I said. "Do you think you'll make it, Elmer?"

The hill was broad and there were no obstructions.

"I'll back her around here and get a new start. These Plymouths'll go anywhere. They're as dependable as jeeps."

Ex-Commodore Wilhelm, sitting in the back seat, leaned over.

"If J. Elmer doesn't upset on the slope of this mountain," he said pessimistically, "he's got something Barney Oldfield lacked."

Elmer not only got us up the hill and parked his car expertly on the down-grade of another and even steeper hill, but also steered a flawless course on the winding, snow-covered walk to the Wohlfarth home.

A home economics major in college, but so gifted at drawing that she was urged to switch courses, Dorothy had master-minded the interior decoration and her eye for simplicity was as evident in her home as was her father's durability in the ring.

"While I was studying home economics," she said, "I decided to apply it, so I got married. By the time the girls were in practice house and studying Child Psych, I had a son of my own and we used him."

Darting upstairs, she was back in a jiffy with Harry Greb Wohlfarth, whose sister Suzanne was too sound asleep to be disturbed. Little Harry, a miniature of his famous grandfather, stood shyly by his grandmother Edwards, in reality his great aunt.

"Harry," Dorothy said, "this is Mr. Fair. You know who he is, don't you?"

Postponing his reply as long as possible, the bashful Harry leaned against his grandmother, then crawled into her lap and kissed her. But he didn't take his eyes off me and when his mother asked again if he knew who I was, he said, "He writes about my Gran'pa."

If the Wohlfarth hospitality did not exceed that of the Edwardses, it certainly equalled it. Dorothy's husband, once an amateur boxer, was doing so much roadwork between the living room and kitchen that I was on the verge of phoning Fritzie Zivic and asking him to come over with the scooter he had snitched from his squawling kid.

At the Edwardses' the night before, Ida had wanted to know about my interview with Tunney last fall. There was an interruption and the matter was forgotten. She brought it up again at Dorothy's.

"What did Gene say about our Harry?') she asked.

"He spoke of him with awesome and loving reverence," I said.

"But he wrote in two of his books that our Harry asked him not to knock him out in their St. Paul fight. Do you think my brother, who never asked favours of opponents and didn't grant many, would have done that?"

"I don't know, but if it wasn't true I think Gene wouldn't have mentioned it because in a sense it was an admission he hadn't done his level-best to win by a knockout, a fact the paying customers wouldn't have appreciated if they had known about it before they bought their tickets. What I do know is that Harry told me Tunney broke two of his ribs, adding, 'I think he carried me for business reasons. Gene was angling for a fight with Tommy Gibbons, who was a spectator and if after what I done to Gibbons, Tunney had knocked me out in front of his eyes, do you think Tommy woulda' give him the match?'"

"Our Harry wouldn't ask anyone not to knock him out," Ida said, "and Tunney had no business saying what he did after my brother's death. Tell him what I said. And if I ever see him I'll tell him myself."

"You wouldn't scratch his eyes out, would you?"

"W—well, maybe not, but I'll tell him off."

Dorothy was sitting across the room and she was smiling.

"If Gene comes to Pittsburgh for the launching of my book, as he has promised he might," I said, "will you help me protect him against Ida? He's still formidable-looking and close to his best fighting weight and he doesn't scare worth a damn, but if Ida ripped into him as your father did, he would feel more comfortable knowing we had been alerted."

"I'll have a talk with her before Gene comes," Dorothy said. "I think I can handle her."

Ida tried to look rambunctious, but her femininity tripped her up. Elmer sat on the edge of the chair, chin high, eyes blinking, hands inverted on his knees. For most of this and the previous evening he had functioned as a tense corroborator of Ida's statements. Now it was time for him to enter the picture.

"One night," Ida said, "our Harry ran into the house after someone—probably a crank—had shot at him. He grabbed Elmer.

"'Elmer,' he said, 'run out there and get into my car and drive away. The dope with the gun will think you're me.'

"Elmer got into the car and drove away and—well, you see him over there natural as life."

Elmer said, "I didn't think about the danger until after I might have been shot."

Always thinking ahead, Elmer was the bright young man who kept training-camp dullness to a minimum. One night when everybody was asleep on the lower floors, he tiptoed up to the third and slammed an automobile tire rim down the steps. Harry Fay, one of Greb's sparring partners, was ghost-shy. He jumped out of a window and fled to the woods.

Greb himself was a prankster. At Manhasset, Long Island, where he was training for one of his title fights, he dressed up like a ghost one midnight and took after Fay, nearly scaring him into insanity. The next night, in KKK garb, he had Fay, still edgy, screaming for help.

A quip artist, Elmer laughs exuberantly when he has been particularly clever. Ex-Commodore Wilhelm asked him if he had ever been told he resembles Churchill. Elmer said he hadn't.

"It's not so much a physical resemblance," Wilhelm said, "but the way you sit in expectancy and the twist you give your phraseology."

Millions of words had been written about the man whose daughter and pet sister were now giving their version of him, but none was as true as those Hemingway jotted down for *Collier's* in 1944 in *London Fights The Robots*:

Mustang is a tough, good name for a bad, tough, husky, angry plane that could have been friends with Harry Greb if Greb had had an engine instead of a heart.

Farther down in that same article, Hemingway, again for comparison, returned to Greb:

Working under censorship is necessary and proper in time of war, and we all censor out ourselves everything we think might be of any possible interest to the enemy. But in writing about the air on the basis of trying to include colour, detail and emotion there is a certain analogy to sports writing.

It is sort of as though in the old days one had found Harry Greb having a breakfast of double orders of ham and eggs and hashed brown potatoes in, bed at nine o'clock in the morning on, the day he was to fight Mickey Walker. Greb, placed on the scales, weighed exactly twelve pounds over the sixty he was to make at two o'clock that afternoon. Now suppose you had seen the weight rubbed and pounded off him and got rid of by several other means and him carried on the scales too weak to walk and almost too weak to curse you.

Then suppose you had seen, the meal he ate and seen him enter the ring weighing exactly the same weight he had left bed with that morning. Then suppose you had seen the great, crowding, smashing, take it, come in again, thumbing, butting, mean, nasty, bloody, lovely fight he made, and you had to sum up the whole business in these terms: one of our fighters named Greb whose characteristics have not been revealed was reported to have encountered an M. Walker last night. Further details will be released in due course...

The sister of a fighter whose colour has inspired our Hemingways and Runyons must frequently drag her mind back to those glorious days when life for him was a carefree skip down a shady lane.

"I'll never forget his return home following a trip to Texas when he was middleweight champion," Ida said. "He had met a girl there, a beauty winner, whom he described as very nice and very pretty but in whom he was not interested."

Greb told Ida the girl just might pop in on her some day. Accustomed to the impromptu visits of his friends, she took the warning as casually as he had sounded it. A week or so later she went to the door and there, surrounded by enough luggage for a touring road show, stood the beauty from Texas.

"She moved right in," Ida said. "I didn't fancy the idea at first, but I saw rather quickly she was a nice kid and I grew fond of her. She helped with the house work, had nice manners and was appreciative. She had had Hollywood ambitions, but evidently they had been dissipated."

Greb came to the house every day or two but he paid almost no attention to the girl.

"She felt badly," Ida said, "but didn't complain. The one day our Harry came in and, bubbling over with enthusiasm told about a party he was arranging at the then Motor Square Hotel. Shyly, as if expecting to be disappointed, she looked up and asked, 'Am I invited?'"

"'Sure, baby' he said, 'the party's for you.'"

More or less managed by Ida, whom Greb always called "the KID," the party was sizable. Ida and Elmer, spatting, were giving each other the raised-shoulder treatment. Greb was dancing with the wife of one of the hotel's proprietors when a gangster moved alongside and tripped her.

"Our Harry hit him so hard," Ida said, "that he landed on his head and shoulders and skidded several feet along the slick dance floor."

The gangster's pals were scattered around the room, but they knew all about Greb's contempt for them and were content to salute and call it a day as far as he was concerned. But if they felt that way about Elmer, their actions didn't prove it. Exiting, one of them banged him on the side of the head with a cuspidor. His left ear, cleanly severed from the top, fell down on his face, held there by only the tiniest speck of the lobe.

"Our Harry and I rushed him to the hospital," Ida said. "Luckily, we had a fine surgeon and he sewed the ear together so well it hardly shows."

Elmer turned his head at an angle to show that the cut was barely noticeable.

It was known among Greb's intimates that he would give them anything he had. And he would fight for any worthy charity, donating his entire purse.

"Every time he had a big-money fight," Ida said, "he sent five hundred dollars to the Immaculate Conception Church in Bloomfield (Pittsburgh). When he had small-money bouts he sent less. Father Bonaventure used to flippantly threaten to break one of the angel statues over our Harry's head for 'short-changing me.' "

Before the first Johnny Wilson fight, Greb, taking life in stride, had ballooned up to what for him was the disproportionate weight of 195 pounds. He would never have gotten the match if Wilson hadn't been convinced it was impossible for anyone to peel down to the middleweight poundage of 160 and retain even a semblance of competent fighting form.

"The day of the fight three weeks later," Ida said, "our Harry jumped on the boxing commission scales and what do you think he weighed? Hundred fifty-eight."

That night, Wilson learned the hard way from Greb about men who could come down from the dreadnaught to the PT class and lose nothing but excess weight.

I told Ida that in an earlier chapter I had castigated newspapermen for writing so many inaccurate stories about Greb, citing as the most ridiculous of all the one about fighting much of his career after the removal of a blind eye (the right) and the substitution of a glass one for it.

"All of us used to wonder how they dreamed that one up," she said. "You know, of course, it wasn't until three months after his retirement from the ring in 1926 that he had his right eye removed."

Some of the misinformation that crept into the stories was not entirely the fault of their authors. Greb usually knew in advance when reporters were going to interview him.

"He would watch for them," Ida said, "and when he saw them he would yell to Elmer or to me to bring him a drink and a cigarette. He would be smoking and drinking when they arrived and their stock question was usually, 'How on earth can you dissipate this way and beat great fighters like Tunney?' "

Greb would shrug his shoulders, empty the glass and order another slug. The reporters didn't know it was just plain unadulterated ginger ale and that he didn't inhale the cigarette smoke, and when they got back to their offices they burned up their typewriters with some of the most readable misinformation ever to reach the nation's press.

"Some of it was awful," Ida said. "Very few reporters knew our Harry personally and some of the stuff their colleagues turned out made us wonder if they had ever seen him in the flesh or known anyone who had."

Stories about Greb's love for the bottle were usually published on the eve of important fights.

"And quite often they produced the desired result," Ida said. "They put him on the short end of the betting and he would wager thousands of dollars on himself to win, sometimes at huge odds."

The Wohlfarth hospitality had just begun to perk when ex-Commodere Wilhelm, who had booked passage on the Trail Blazer, said it was time to leave. The Edwardses carried us back to the William Penn, carried being an apt description in my case.

"I'll mail you a copy of this chapter when it's written," I told Ida, not foreseeing then that it was going to end on the order of a Pepys' Diary. "Make any changes you deem advisable. It will be the only pre-publication chapter you will have read and I want you to have your say."

I mailed it to her and she returned it with minor changes. After expressing general approval in an accompanying letter and flattering me with a liberal scattering of literary orchids, she came in fast with her Sunday punch.

"But please say," she wrote, "that I still have not read your book ...and the Lord above only knows what I will think of you when I do, for deep down inside of me I feel there must be a bit of scoundrel in you, because I am as ignorant now about its contents as I was when I first met you...."

Dorothy, who hadn't previously read the Esquire anthology article about her father, read it and then she read a copy of the chapter I had sent Ida.

"I read them both," she wrote, "not once but many times. I'll have to admit that I felt very squeamish about the eye gouging part of The Iron City Express, but Phil (her husband) informed me it was downright silly to feel that way about it. He explained that e.g. (I don't even like to write it) was a sort of boxing technique and more or less generally practised. Anyhow— after being convinced about that point —I thought The Iron City Express was very much O.K. And the chapter also met with my heartiest approval,"

Chapter XIII

A Warrior's Pilot

Except for two short intervals when he gave way to George Engel and James J. Johnston, Red Mason was Greb's lifelong manager. Swashbuckling and alert, he haunted sports editors, employing every artifice with which to stampede them into keeping the names of his fighters before the public. If the sports departments were closed when he made his nocturnal calls he would get in if he had to jimmy the doors, bang out a fairly comprehensive release and leave it on the sports editors' typewriters. If one of his fighters forsook him for another manager, Mason corralled reporters and, gesticulating like a madman, told them "That guy is a dog (meaning a quitter), and an ingrate." If a week or a year later—it didn't matter how long he had been away—he returned to the fold, Mason, as warm in praise as he had been sour in condemnation, told reporters, "He's the gamest and most appreciative fighter I ever owned."

When one of his fighters was taking a pasting, Mason would yell an unending assortment of foul names at his opponent, who complained that "When you fight Mason's fighters you have to fight Mason too." If name-calling failed to retard the paster, Mason scooted around the ring and started a fight with his manager. There sometimes was the unusual spectacle of Mason's fighter getting the massaging of his life and Mason thumping the gizzard out of the opposition manager under the latter's corner.

One night, unable to dislodge the opposition's concentration on his fighter's mid-section by baiting him, Mason switched to Jimmy Diamond in the other corner. Diamond owned a big stable of boxers and he worked them out of New Castle, Pa. After yelling hideous names until the emanations from his throat were dry wheezes, Mason was reliably informed that Diamond was totally deaf. From then until he went to his happy hunting ground he carried a card index in which he listed the condition of opposition managers' auditory nerves.

If a Mason fighter had been unable to get down to the stipulated poundage at weigh-in time - well, there was that day in an Ohio town a decade ago.

Buck Crouse, now a Pittsburgh referee, was to work in the main bout. He couldn't make the weight. Posing as Crouse, Al Grayber, one of Greb's sparring partners, stepped on the scales. Ten pounds lighter, he made the poundage at which Crouse, who was going to do the fighting that night, had agreed to make. It was all very slick until boxing officials got wise and, as a member of that entourage said on a recent lecture tour, "Throwed Mason and all of us tigers out of town."

Another Mason trick, usually successful, was to stick a wad of chewing gum on a coin and then stick them onto the weight ring of the old-fashioned Fairbanks scales on which, in those lovely, larcenous days, fighters were weighed in. It cut ten pounds off a pug's weight.

"If it can be done as fast today and with as little privation to the weight-shedder," noted Whitey Bimstein as he tutored his brave Rocky Graziano in the more velvety art of fisticuffing, "there's plenty of dames in Hollywood who would go far and do much for the man who showed them the light."

During Greb's and Mason's early association Greb was so small that he didn't dare get on the scales in front of boxing officials when he was fighting towering giants. But these mirthful troubadours had to eat. And to make sure they ate well they sometimes carried a "spare," a heavyweight who weighed in for Greb and then left town. The deception was always discovered in the dressing room before ringtime.

"But there wasn't much boxing officials could do," said Happy Albacker, "with the 'spare' waitin' in another city to repeat the performance a couple of days later, so Greb was permitted to fight. It wasn't nothin' for him to be outweighed sixty-five pounds. Naturally, he won easy, we all ate well and everybody was happy but the unlucky gink which tangled with our ferocious little cub."

Greb used to taper off training by playing a sizzling handball game with Mason. With only one eye - and by no means a good eye - he either had to follow the ball by instinct or run in on it so fast he was close enough to hit it when it bounced off the backboard. Watching him, Philadelphia Jack O'Brien himself a good speed merchant and old-time fistic great, once said, "He's the fastest human on the getaway I ever saw. He can loaf and still outrun Paddock for a hundred yards. I'm sure of that."

Greb lost to as often as he won from Mason. And as of the first day they competed against each other it was an accepted rule that the loser pick up that evening's dinner check. But Mason, an uncanny finagler, usually euchered Greb into such an awkward position that he had to pay to avoid public embarrassment, regardless of whose turn it was.

One evening Greb, Albacker and Mason were boarding a train in Chicago. The head of the redcaps stopped Albacker.

"What's wrong with the Champ?" he asked. "He never gives no mo' than a dime tip. Dempsey gives two dollahs."

Mr. Albacker asked Greb about it.

"That chiselin' two-bit pimp!" Greb roared. "He's been puttin' two dollars for tips on the expense account for redcaps ever since we've been together."

Handing Mr. Albacker a five-dollar bill with instructions to give it to the redcaps' chief, he took after Mason.

"I could tell by the way he was holdin' his suitcase over his head he wasn't imitatin' Atlas holdin' the world up," Mr. Albacker remarked concretely. "As Mason tried to duck into a berth Harry slugged him with that wardrobe. The way he looked when I picked him up several hours later was so humorous I'm still laughin' about it."

Would Mr. Albacker elaborate on what made Mason look so humorous?

"With pleasure. Take a pickle which has no juice in it. It's dried up, ain't it? Well, there was considerable seepage from that slug on the bean and Mason looked like a dried-up pickle."

One of Mason's fighters, a young Jewish boy, was working in a bout in Wheeling. When he came back to his corner at the end of the first round he said, with typical racial characteristic shrugging of shoulders and moving of head, "Oy, oy, can that guy hit!"

Mason didn't say anything.

At the end of each round the youthful Jew made the same comment and with identical results—no reply from Mason. Returning to his corner at the end of the next to last round, he tried again for a sympathetic response from his manager—"Oy, oy, can that guy hit!" When Mason still refused to be drawn out, his fighter looked up pleadingly, unhappily.

"But you don't care, do you Mr. Mason?" he sighed.

Then there was the time Mason made another trip to Wheeling with his fighters, one of whom fell ill. This man, a middleweight, had a name as Irish as Paddy McGurk. Substituting for him and using the same Irish name was a Negro water-bucket boy, as black a man as ever lived. A raw novice, he was floored so often and by so many varieties of sucker punches that the customers were imploring the referee to stop the uneven contest. As he left his corner for the final round, his face a lumpy, bloody smear, Mason told him, "All you've got to do to win now, Hambone, is knock him out."

"Sho' 'nuf?" spat the Negro, his spirit fired by Mason's attempt at persiflage.

"Positively, Hambone. Knock him out and you win."

The Negro threw his right hand as if he never wanted to see it again. It landed squarely on the button, winning by a sensational knockout for the crude Mason entry a fight that should have been given to his opponent on a technical knockout in any but the last and, for him, unlucky round.

New Yorkers called Mason First Offer Mason and a clunk. He did accept the first offer made for the services of his pugs, but he kept them busy and in tiptop physical condition, was careful not to over-match them and far from being a clunk, or bonehead, he was a brilliant psychologist.

The night of Cuddy DeMarco's first fight with Jack Zivic, Cuddy's dark countenance, as he sat in his dressing room awaiting the call to the ring, was wrapped in nervous anxiety. Jack was a hitter from hell. Cuddy's hands were taped and he was working his fingers and adjusting the tape before putting his gloves on. A big, brusque man with a Slavic accent stormed in.

"Take the tape off, you idiot," he thundered. "No tape allowed tonight."

Mason grabbed-the crass intruder and, screaming hysterically, started a fight with him. Cuddy jumped up and stopped it.

"I didn't know until later," he said, "that it was a gag. Mason had arranged it with Luke Barnett (Pittsburgh's nationally known professional practical joker) as an antidote to my tenseness. It loosened me up and I turned in one of my best fights."

Mason was resourceful in other directions, too. He was in Johnstown with his stable of fighters who were to box in the ball park. Word got around that the promoter was going to skip town without paying for the bouts. But he would wait until Mason was busy swinging the towel and imparting advice in the corner. Then he would scurry into the ticket office, pick up the black satchel containing the money and hightail it for distant Darts.

Now it was more or less conservative enterprise in those buccaneering, dog-eat-dog days for promoters to short-change prizefighters and their managers. But to scramble out of town without so much as giving them carfare back home was considered unethical in the trade. In Mason's card index it was more than that. Listed under C (for chicanery), it was "stinking, lowdown and underhanded" and demanded such radical countermeasures as to teach an object lesson. Clipping his red hair so short that a cap would cover it, and grabbing the recently shedded clothes of a ballpark flunky, Mason strode boldly into the ticket office, picked up the satchel in which every last dollar had been neatly packed, and hot-footed it down the mountain for home. Behind him he left (1) his fighters, who not only had to play nursemaid to one another during the bouts but also borrow carfare home, and (2) a Promoter who regretted he had waited for the last dollar to come through the ticket window before leaving.

In Pittsburgh's nearby McKeesport the fans used to stomp their feet and yell, just before the main bout started, "Speech! Speech! We want Mason !') He always responded and always got his big ears booed off. Then one night he was in Youngstown, where his speech-making capacity had preceded him, and the fans, as the flashy, slashing windmill that was Greb jumped through the ropes, yelled "Speech! Speech! We want Mason!" They got him. And instead of booing him they cheered him. He doubted their sincerity. No matter how arduously they urged him on subsequent visits with his terrific tiger, he never made another speech in Youngstown.

"I prefer the boos of McKeesport to the cheers of Youngstown,"

It was in McKeesport that he developed the technique of spraying his fighters with mouthfuls of water as they came back to their corners, and socking the knockdown timekeeper's bell with a water bottle without detection, prematurely ending the round and giving his fighters the advantage of an illicit rest when they needed it most. In McKeesport, Mason was almost as big attraction as his fighters and when the fans called for a speech they got it, regardless of how lustily they had booed his last one.

Greb kept an eye—a jaundiced eye—on Mason most of the time, but it wasn't always sharp enough. In Hot Springs a year or so before Greb's retirement, Mason handed him a paper and asked him to sign it. Greb wanted to know what it was and Mason said, "Application for renewal of your boxing license." Greb signed it without reading it only to learn it was not as stated but, according to informed sources, a renewal of his contract with Mason calling for a 13½ per cent increase over the old one. Greb raised his eyebrows when he heard about it. He raised them higher when, finally getting hold of the contract, close scrutiny revealed a lot of whereases, and/ors and other legal phraseology that redounded to Mason's but not Greb's benefit. He refused to abide by it. Mason took him to court, but the case was thrown out. There was considerable bickering after that, with Greb ignoring Mason's demands and giving him what he saw fit. He was not over-fond of managers, anyhow, his optimistic faith in them seldom getting beyond the stage of permitting them to carry his baggage. Nevertheless, he kept Mason with him until the gong ended the last smashing, bruising, vicious round of his last fight in 1926.

Chapter XIV

The Angels Got Big Bill First

He was a notorious in-and-outer—great today, stinking tomorrow. But he was big and tough and awfully wise and for eleven-rounds, according to my score card, he was heavyweight champion of the world.

He had an incentive that night twenty-six years ago. Two years earlier, in 1918, a biff on the chin had turned him around so that when he fell one of his legs doubled up under him and an ankle snapped. But despatches out of Milwaukee the next day told a somewhat different story - a story seasoned, it later developed, to its author's taste. They said that chin-wallop was no ordinary affair but one that carried so much power the shock, like electricity, travelled down the frame and broke the walloppee's leg. He hadn't forgotten those stories and now, two years later, he was fighting a second time the man whose shrewd manager had fed those twisted versions to the press. Only this time, up there in the old Madison Square Garden ring, a well conditioned challenger was pitted against a recently crowned champion who had held him too lightly.

Down in the press section we could hear Big Bill Brennan, fresh and unmarked, sneering insults at Jack Dempsey, winded, an ear torn, bleeding from the mouth. Coming out for the twelfth, Dempsey was himself again, a fleet, crouching, weaving menace of the roped square. So fast the eye could hardly follow it, Dempsey crashed a destructive fist against the jaw and while Brennan was falling, wheeled and walked away. When Brennan got up the fight was over and Dempsey, a towel around his head, was leaving the ring.

Big, soft-hearted, rough and comical, Bill Brennan departed this transient world a short time later. At Stillman's they say he was handling the gate on St. Peter's day off and when Greb presented himself for admittance-no recommendations were necessary. But before he ran into a bullet from a fleeing thug's gun, Brennan had done a heap of huffing and puffing against the Iron City Express. In Pittsburgh for one of these reunions, which, incidentally, bore not the slightest resemblance to pat-a-cake, he cornered sportswriter Harry Keck.

"I'm gonna knock your boy loose from his can this time," Brennan said. "I've been laying awake at nights figgerin' and figgerin' and now it's all figgered out. I'm not gonna scatter my punches like I've been doin', tryin' to punch it out with him. This time I'm gonna wait for an openin'—let the fans boo all they want to while I wait—and when I get it, whoppo! and there'll be Greb deader'n a mackerel on the door. That little piddle pot ain't big enough to stand up under one of my socks if I nail him right."

Brennan fought as be said he would. He didn't throw a punch, but stood there catching them while the fans booed him for his inactivity. His chance came in the fifth and he rifled a right to the chin. It was a gorgeous straight rhythmical thing with two hundred and ten pounds of nurtured bitterness behind it. It lifted Greb off his feet and slung him into the ropes so hard that a ring post flew out of its mooring. Greb ricocheted off and flew back to the attack, hitting from every angle and with every variety of punch known to man. Brennan tried desperately to stem the torrent that swirled about him and when everything else failed, he wrapped his forearms around his face and glued his elbows to his chest. Moving his head around and peering through the latticework of fingers over eyes, he tried to keep abreast of Greb's movements. There weren't any maps to show Greb where were located unexposed areas of the body he loved to punch, but instinct directed him to the rear. Brennan zig-zagged and turned around, but Greb was in step and he serenaded him with a deafening barrage of open glove smacks from the head down to and including the rump. Harry Keck went back to Brennan's dressing room after the fight.

"Well, Big Bill," he said, "you had your chance in the fifth."

"No use denyin' I didn't," Brennan said through puffed lips that looked like bleeding toadstools, "and it was the saddest thing that ever happened to me."

Three months later, or less than a year before he was to give Dempsey such a miserable evening, Brennan was back in Pittsburgh for another Greb fight. Eddie Deasy stopped him. Though Deasy was Greb's friend, he was also close to Brennan. "What kinda shape you in?" Deasy asked.

"Wonderful," Brennan said, "You've got to be in perfect condition to fight that little bastard, but I'll tell you confidentially, Eddie—if Dempsey was fightin' that buzz-saw instead of me, I would bet on Greb."

At six o'clock that evening Brennan was having dinner at Harry Kramer's restaurant, now the Hofbrau.

"Big Bill," Kramer said, "I see by the papers that you're fighting our little man again. According to my statistics, you didn't do so good against him in Syracuse, Tulsa and here. How do you figure to do?"

Brennan took a side of beef out of his mouth and draped it care fully around a baked potato.

"How," he asked resignedly, "does anybody figger to do with that little mule? You go in there and catch 'em"—here he punched his face and body to exemplify—"and that's all there is to it, just go in there and catch 'em."

And that was exactly what he did—210-pound Brennan against 155-pound Greb.

In his heyday Eddie Deasy hobnobbed with the upper, middle and lower levels—from Warren G. Herding down the line to Arnold Rothstein and dollar-a-crack whores. Someplace in between was Daddy Browning, the wealthy New York realtor whose hobbies were honking ganders, high-school cuties and rented Rolls Royces; and the comedienne, now famous but still friendly, who piled onto a Beauty Rest and made four of Pittsburgh's best men yell Uncle during a brief train stopover one morning.

"Clever woman, a stylist," Deasy said.

Deasy's idol was Greb.

"I can't think about him without crying," he said, throwing down a double rye in a saloon just off Pittsburgh's Diamond.

Tall and limber, he sauntered up nearby Fifth Avenue, crossing at intervals to stand by or near a landmark - always a landmark that brought back memories of Greb. He stopped in a Smithfield Street bar. Wherever he went he was hailed by someone who knew him when he was rolling around the country with Greb, and always the subject was Greb - Greb who has been dead twenty years.

"Pittsburgh," he said, "is one of the world's best fight towns. No other city three times its size has turned out half as many ring stars."

But Greb was its all-time great - not only Pittsburgh's but the world's. It wasn't until he was getting along in years that he grew into a full-blown middleweight. Few men his size would fight him, and the ones who did came off as badly as did Mickey Walker, then in his prime, against Greb, then an old man. Currently, when a middleweight spots an opponent ten pounds he has to get special dispensation from the boxing commission. But when Greb was down for a bout with an opponent who outweighed him thirty to sixty pounds, boxing commissioners stroked their beards and philosophised that it was none of their business if this was the bigger man's method of getting himself whittled down to a midget.

Approaching the William Penn, Deasy, still pointing out landmarks, levelled his cane.

"And here," he said, "is what another generation of Pittsburghers used to call Virgin Alley."

"How did it get its nickname?" I asked.

Before Deasy could answer, a kibitzer from behind answered for him: "Neutral territory for girls when Greb was on the prowl."

Whether Deasy heard it was not indicated by his actions. He cocked his head like an old rooster about to preen himself, shook his cane and squinted.

"It was Cherry Way," he said, "before it was renamed Oliver Avenue."

Deasy and Greb used to take the baths together at Hot Springs, Arkansas. En route to nearby Eldorado for an exhibition one day Greb, ill from food poisoning, was vomiting. Looking up, he noticed birds flying low over their open car. They were big birds and he wanted to know what kind they were.

"Turkey buzzards," Deasy said, explaining that they belonged to the vulture family.

Greb jerked back.

"I'll never forget the frightened look in his eyes," Deasy said. "It was as if a voice of an unseen man had told him the end was near."

Deasy, in whose eyes is the twinkle of a county fair barker, has been fuming for years over the article Quentin Reynolds wrote for Collier's in which he told about Greb and Mickey Walker having engaged in a street fight a few hours after their ring classic.

"When I read that piece," he said, "I wondered why I hadn't seen the brawl or heard about it. Another thing that puzzled me was how in God's name, with this thing happening in the Times Square district, did the newspapers miss it?"

"Maybe," I said, "the late man on the city desk and his rewrite man were too busy playing poker to bother with it. Maybe, too, they were whooping it up at Bleeck's (Artists.& Writers Restaurant), where, after exposure to the likes of Luscious Bebee and prohibition hootch, the matter of two famous world's champions battling it out in the street seemed unimportant.

"I'll donate a thousand dollars to any worthwhile charity," Deasy said, his Adam's apple playing tag with his tongue, "if anyone who claims he saw that street fight can prove it to the satisfaction of an impartial judge."

"Don't write about me," entreated my friend of thirty years. "If you do people will think you're my press agent." He didn't say, and I didn't ask, if it was all right to write about him if I omitted his name.

He has never had a boxing glove on his hands, yet few boxers know as much about fistic styles and how to combat them. Strong water has never flown past his lips, and he doesn't smoke, chew tobacco, rub snuff, belittle competitors or ask girls how about it. But despite these unenviable virtues, he has a sinner's zest for life and is patient as Job, as witness:

One afternoon Professor William McCarney, then a silent partner in Max Schmeling's ownership, was guzzling some of his property's Scotch at Madame Bey's training camp. I asked the Professor, a robust and heroic gentleman who has stood when others have fallen, if he had seen my old friend in recent months.

"I was over there with some of my meat eaters not long ago," he said, "and I dropped around to his office. As I was leaving after a long, intimate and pleasant visit, I asked him what he thought of the bouts I was going to put on two days hence.

"'Professor,' he said, 'I love you personally, but your meat eaters are so rancid they'll smell out the joint and my story, which runs in tomorrow's paper, will say so.'"

My old friend, whose stories start parading into his office at the crack of dawn and are telling themselves long after midnight, first met Greb when Greb was a kid.

"I'll never forget Harry standing there by my desk holding his cap," he said. "Modest and shy, he looked as young as he really was. Yet over in Philadelphia he had been kicking the hell out of seasoned, hard-fighting men like Billy Miske, Mike Gibbons, George Chip and Jack Blackburn, the cagey old fox who was later to tutor Joe Louis into fame.'"

.He was in Youngstown the day Greb fought, and whipped, Joe Chip, by whom he once had been technically knocked out. A woman fight fan grabbed Greb in the hotel lobby and, gushing, said it was terrific meeting him.

"You got the wrong party, lady," Greb said. "If you're lookin' for Harry Greb the fighter, right over there he is." He pointed to my old friend who looked about as much like Greb as Harvey the rabbit. The woman ran over and greeted him.

"What a frustrated old blister!" he said. "If she hadn't been, Greb would have told her to take her place—and don't shove, please!—in the line that was already forming in the vicinity of his suite."

Though he knew him as few men did, perforated in his memory is the way Greb came into the ring.

"Light of foot, knees high," he said, "Harry pranced in like a yearling. You felt that his only worry was whether he could hold himself in check until the gong turned him loose."

After winning Tunney's American light-heavyweight title, Greb spent more time than usual in New York. One day back home he told a reporter that the old town had changed a lot.

"In what way?" the reporter asked.

"The buildings are smaller and the sidewalks narrower."

"You're pretty sure about that?"

"No doubt about it, they've shrunk."

After losing his title to Tiger Flowers, Greb ran into the same reporter.

"It's nice," he said, "to be back home among old friends. They're the ones who are with you whether you win or lose."

"How about the buildings and the sidewalks?" the reporter reminded him.

"They were smaller and narrower the last time I saw you."

"Dammit," Greb stiffened, "don't you guys never take your brains out of gear?"

A species of publicity-seeking celebrities sought to attract attention to themselves by trying to run away with Greb after some of his spectacular fights. They didn't try it a second time. His friends, save for a few men like Douglas Fairbanks, Sr., were men who believed in him when he was punching his way up the long, narrow, mean pugilistic trail. When he was being feted, it was with these men - cabbies, flunkies, bellhops - with whom he shared the limelight. Following a fight in Cincinnati with Jeff Smith, a telegram from Pittsburgh informed him that an old friend, a bootlegger, had been convicted and sentenced to serve a term in a Federal penitentiary in Illinois.

"We'll hurry back home," Greb told Happy Albacker, "and go with him as far as Chicago."

Opinion is divided as to who blinded Greb in his right eye. Some say Jeff Smith did it, but Ida Edwards says it was Rid Norfolk.

Among Greb's friends were some mighty imperturbable characters. One of them staggered into a Pittsburgh hotel following the last Greb-Gibbons fight.

In the elevator he handed an unsealed, unstamped envelope to the bellhop. Remembering it the next morning, he phoned the bellhop.

"Did you keep that envelope for me?"

"I thought you meant for me to throw it away," the bellhop said, "so-I throwed it down the laundry chute."

"See if you can't fish it out," Greb's buddy said placidly.

The bellhop found it and returned it. In it, mostly in five hundred and thousand-dollar bills, was one hundred forty thousand dollars.

"I didn't have no complaint with the reward I got," the bellhop said. "In one fight; that man has had enough money on Greb's nose to finance a chain of harems."

In Atlantic City where he was training for his first Tunney fight in 1926, Jack Dempsey offered Greb a thousand dollars a day to put him in condition for the bout. Greb, who had retired from the ring two months before, turned it down.

"I would feel like a burglar takin' Jack's money," he said. "Nobody can get him in good enough condition to whip Gene."

James J. Johnston, the quondam Boy Bandit, remembers Greb as a restless, energetic, impulsive athlete.

"Harry," he said, "was sitting on my desk in my office when I came in one day. He fancied himself a wrestler and clamped a leg scissors on me. I figure I gotta humour him, but I never expected him to rip all the ligaments off five ribs. Fortunately, though, he didn't put the squeeze on my writing hand and hence I was able to sign him to a contract."

Summing up the Greb-Ted Moore Milk Fund fight at Yankee Stadium in 1924 - Greb's middleweight title was at stake and he retained it with ease - one New York reporter wrote, "Greb has satisfied everybody that he can fight cleanly and with observance of the rules."

"Do you know Jack?" (Dempsey), Tunney asked the afternoon we spent at El Charro, the tiny Mexican restaurant in Greenwich Village where he painstakingly taught Jose de Paz how to pour wine without spilling a drop.

"I worked all of his title fights," I said, "except two - Gibbons in Shelby and yours in Chicago -and I've met him, but I don't know him."

"A wonderful fellow," Tunney said. "You'll talk with him before finishing your book, of course."

"I want to," I said, and changed the subject without saying why I wasn't going to. The reason is simple. He and Greb were matched by Charley Murray of Buffalo, but the match was called off and Greb sort of blamed the old Mauler. Dempsey is noted for his long memory for faces and I seem to recall being with Greb when they met one day. Greb glanced up. "Hey, bum," he said roguishly, "when you gonna fight me?" I've been a little jittery ever since and saw no reason for agitating this condition by being identified as a chum of the man who even in jest had the temerity to call the great Demps a bum.

When Greb was coming up and Jack Johnson was going down they boxed a four-round exhibition in Kid Howard's gymnasium in Chicago.

"It was a pleasure workin' with you, Jack," Greb said, and Johnson, the first Negro to hold the heavyweight championship, said, "It's almost impossible to set you up for a punch. You're the fastest man I ever boxed."

When Dempsey and Greb were in their prime—Dempsey weighing around 185, Greb someplace between 150-155 - speculation was rife as to the outcome if they had fought each other. Both were roughhousers who eschewed boxing rules. Dempsey followers contended he would have caught up with the flashy Greb and flattened him some time after the tenth, when he would have begun to tire. Greb followers nearly choked with laughter at such reasoning, maintaining that he didn't really shift into high until after the tenth.

With justifiable sisterly pride, Ida Edwards said, "Our Harry would have whipped Dempsey." Whether or not Dempsey felt that way, Jack Kearns, his manager, did. In the training ring he had seen Greb open a long gash over one of Dempsey's eyes and cuff him around with gay abandon. Not once but every time they worked together, he had seen Greb outspeed, outslug and outthink his meal ticket and on at least two occasions Kearns had stopped the uneven proceedings and thrown Greb out of the ring for being too rough.

Speed Layman, current trainer of West Virginia's Golden Gloves team, used to work out with Greb, and he and his younger brother, Kid Layman, have boxed each other on Greb cards out in the sticks.

"Greb usually had twenty expensive suits of clothes," he said, "and two girls for each suit."

Bill Bess, who originated West Virginia's Golden Glovers and whose publisher, the Huntington Advertiser, sponsors them, saw Greb box Chuck Wiggins at Clyffeside Park between Huntington (W. Va.) and Ashland, Kentucky. Young Bess had associated boxing with fencing - a gentleman's sport in which conformity to the rules was as paramount as skill itself. And he had no reason to change this impression when, after the fighters had entered the ring, Dr. C.M. Hawes, referee, speaking through a megaphone, asked permission from the spectators to shorten the fight from twelve to ten rounds on grounds of a slim attendance.

"Mister Greb and Mister Wiggins," the referee said, "are performing for a tenth of what they would get in Pittsburgh or New York. I paid to get in here the same as you did, but I'm willing to shorten it if you are."

The spectators gave their consent, and the fight went on.

"Jehoshaphat!" Bill Bess exclaimed, "but Mister Greb and Mister Wiggins re-educated me fast. Butting, heeling, back-handing, elbowing, thumbing, kicking, biting, cursing - why, man, I get the creeps recalling how ungentlemanly those gentlemen were to each other."

No hocus-pocus about it, when that pair locked horns there were no Gaston-Alphonse punctilios.

"But after their Clyffeside fight," Bess said, "they wrapped their arms around each other in fond embrace and left town together as happy as two crazy zombies."

In the musical comedy, Plain Little Jane, was a routine theatrical boxing skit. In it, also, was Louise Walton, a cutie pants. Greb followed the touring company from town to town and when he was asked one day why he did this he said, "It's because of that boxing skit. Every time I see it I learn plenty.

One day Greb handed a girl over to Happy Albacker.

· "Take her," he said, "to that hair dresser in the Jenkins Arcade and bring her back (to the Colonial Hotel) when she's finished."

A brunette when Mr. Albacker took her, she was a blonde when he handed her back to Greb.

"Greb didn't like her at all that way," Mr. Albacker said, "and waved her away, tellin' me to take her to her husband in Wilkinsburg.'" Did Mr. Albacker do it?

"Would you a-did it if you knowed her husband, was settin' at home waitin' to wrap a lead pipe around any man's dome which he saw her with?"

Some weeks after boxing Jimmy Delaney in Pittsburgh Greb boxed him in St. Paul. Delaney and his manager, Mike Collins, came into Greb's dressing room to inspect his bandaged hands.

"How'ya, Harry?" Collins asked cheerily.

"Don't how'ya me," Greb howled. "Your bum"? - Delaney was not a bum but a good enough fighter to go ten rounds twice with Tunney - "hit me in the balls in Pittsburgh and there wasn't no excuse for it. I'm warnin' you," snarled the roughest, toughest, most courageous fighter I ever saw, "that I'm not gonna be responsible for what happens to him if he does it again."

Arthur Daley, in his Sports of the Times column, printed a letter from a reader several years ago which read in part. ... "Your reference to Harry Greb in the column on Gene Tunney made me wonder why no one has written a really good history of Greb's career. For a man who fought in three weight classes and tossed his opponents around in all three, about the only time he gets attention is when someone more famous remembers when he was pasted by Greb."

Home on leave from the navy, Greb offered to box a four-round exhibition under sponsorship of Pittsburgh sports editors who were raising money to buy tobacco for service men in the first world war. A week before the bout no opponent had stepped up. Frank Klaus heard about it and offered his services.

"But," said Harry Keck, in charge of the benefit, "you've been out of the ring six years. You can't get in shape in time."

"I'll go on the road tomorrow morning," said Klaus, who once fought Stanley Ketchel to a standstill in a no-decision bout and later held the middleweight title, "and I'll be ready in time."

Five days later he was in the ring with Greb. Instead of boxing an exhibition they tried to kill each other. And there was little choice between them when it was all over. Twenty-three years later, or the night Fritzie Zivic knocked out Henry Armstrong, Klaus was telling sculptress Challis Walker and me about that exhibition. Greb had come into Klaus' dressing room before they were called into the ring.

"We'll use these tonight, Frank," he said, handing Klaus a pair of heavily padded training gloves.

"What a sweet gesture," Miss Walker said.

Klaus nudged me in the ribs.

"Your doll," he said, "is a little innocent, ain't she?"

Then he leaned over. "Lady," he said, "it was not a sweet gesture, it was a cute gesture. Those big pillows, the way Greb intended using them, would have ripped the skin off my tender face. When I told him to go fly his kite, that we would use regulation small gloves, he gave me a hurt look calculated to make me feel I was a heel for seeing through his premeditated plan to skin me alive."

Record books list Greb as having engaged in some two hundred sixty fights, but this isn't half of them. In one busy year he fought more than Joe Louis has fought in his entire career. The reason so many of his bouts weren't listed was that during his early days he fought so often that no one in his camp bothered to notify record book publishers.

Greb always had cold hands, even in the summer.

"Had you noticed?" I asked Tunney after congratulating him for his part in the Reader's Digest's recently published round table discussion on exercise.

"No," he said.

"His daughter Dorothy has cold hands too."

"How do you know?" Tunney cleared his throat suggestively.

"I held them and I told her her pa always had cold hands."

"Where was Dorothy's husband?" Tunney ahem'd.

"Right there at the table in the Pittsburgh Playhouse," I said. "He regarded it as part of the interview."

Chapter XV

Not an Inhibition Between Them

Greb was boxing Kid Norfolk in Boston and Happy Albacker was walking down to the ring with him.

"Listen, Hap," Greb said quietly, "you got a heavy load o' laughin' water aboard tonight and you better not work in my corner. I don't wanna listen to drunken talk, understand, Hap? You know what a puncher this jig is, and he's bigger'n I am, so I got you a seat over there in the front row. Okay, Hap?"

"Sure, anything you say. I'll set over there and pray for you."

"Pray hard because I'll need the Lord on my side."

For years Kid Norfolk had called himself the Black Thunderbolt and Negro Light-heavyweight Champion and he had stood up admirably under this self-billing. For years, too, his magnificent bows from the ring had made him the envy of less limber fistic brethren. And outside the ring he had draped long arms around many a cuddly ebony dazzler anxious to live up to his expectations. A capable fighter before the years slowed him down, he couldn't be propagandised into defeat the way Max Beer was prior to the Louis fight. When Battling Siki came to this country after electrifying the world by knocking out the Lily of France, otherwise Georges Carpentier, in Paris, the old Kid took him on in Madison Square Garden and all but burned him at the stake. The Kid fought Harry Wills, too, and his work was praiseworthy until he went down from a pop atop his closely-sheared head - a head that, according to informed sources, had once caught a series of wallops by an enthusiastic crowbar wielder-without, showing signs of cleavage. He stayed down for the count and then, full of fight, jumped up mumbling "Whar dat man?" A number of the boys in the press section thought it was a trained seal act and held their noses until the wind changed.

Greb had learned about the Kid the hard way. He hadn't seen anything to be gained in boxing him that first time in Pittsburgh, but when the match was made he went through with it. Before the fight, he had said, "If the going gets tough, I'll stick my thumb in his eye." The going got tough and he stuck his thumb in the Kid's eye. The Kid reciprocated with the Norfolk thumb, blinding Greb in the right eye.

Greb was doing all right in their next fight - this one in Boston - but no better than all right. As he had said, the Kid was considerably larger, a stiff hitter, and he was a cute old codger to boot.

"I don't know where that bottle comes from," Mr. Albacker said, "but suddenly I've got a quart of whiskey in my hand, and I'm already loaded with tiger juice, and what I don't need is a quart of whiskey. So I climb over the press benches to the ring. Harry thinks I want to tell him somethin'. He wheels the Kid over toward where I'm standin'. Just then the bell rings for the end of the round and I tell him to hit him—hit him after the bell. Greb hits him and the Kid hits him back. I seen red, Jim. I'm tellin' you, I seen red. Imagine the Kid sockin' my pal after the bell, away up there in Boston so far from home!"

When Mr. Albacker has seen red he has been known to act impulsively.

"I bounce that quart off the Kid's cranium," he said uproariously. "And what do you think them puritanical New Englanders do? The Massachusetts Boxin' Commission hands Harry and the Kid suspensions for fightin' after the bell."

That thump on Br'er Norfolk's cranium must have opened it up so wide the machinery was exposed.

"Not a bit of it," Mr. Albacker assured with the comforting air of a fraudulent stock salesman. "They made tough heads in them days. Besides, the Kid was so busy tryin' to defend himself he didn't even notice it."

In Pittsburgh one rainy night Greb told a cab driver to take him to Curley Leacock's roadhouse.

"Don't waste no time," he said caustically, "and don't hit every bump in the road either."

Before he had closed the door the cab jerked, dumping him into the seat. Then the driver zig-zagged all over the bumpy road, hitting every bump in it. Next, he stopped short, almost plunging Greb through the partition into the driver's compartment. Greb cursed. "Okay, wise guy, get out!" the driver snarled.

Greb jumped out and started to pull the driver out. Having pulled his cap down over his eyes, the driver pushed it up again.

"Why Hap!" Greb whooped. "I been tryin' to find you for two weeks. Where you been?"

Mr. Albacker had been on a toot. Coming off sorely pressed for jingling money and not wanting to mooch off his pal, he had gone back to hacking.

"Leave this trouble buggy here," Greb said, "and come home with me.

He left the cab there in the middle of the road, hailed another one and went home with Greb.

In Atlantic City one night Greb suddenly missed Mr. Albacker. After making the rounds of likely hangouts without turning up a clue, he remembered Joe's Rainbow Garden. He found him there, full of prohibition hootch and in a waiter's uniform singing Fortune Teller Man. Mr. Albacker's halting voice and uncertain footing were bringing the house down, but Greb didn't think it was funny. Like a proud mother and with a mother's humility, he pleaded with him to go home.

"I kept singin' my old favourite," Mr. Albacker said, "until I noticed the mother look fadin' from Harry's eyes. Drunk as I was, I knew it was time to retire."

Greb took him to their suite and left him there. Then he went back to Joe's Rainbow Garden and—

"He didn't kill Joe," Mr. Albacker said soothingly, "but I always had the idea that the reason he didn't was because Joe saw him comin' and lammed it out of there on a rocket for the moon."

There was just one Challenger Greb shied from - John Barleycorn.

"You can't whip him, Hap," he used to say.

But Mr. Albacker was always in there trying.

"Harry," he said, "has had me in almost every alcoholic institution in the East. I'll never forget how he lectured me against drinkin'. And when the lectures were over, he'd say, 'Hap, I would provide for you in my will, but any galoot knows I'll outlive you by half a century.' "

Came a golden October afternoon - a caressingly warm day with a lullaby in the cloudless sky. Greb was telling Mr. Albacker of plans to open a business men's gymnasium in downtown Pittsburgh. He was through fighting now (aged thirty-two) and all the glitter and acclaim of a great champion - in his case twice a champion - were behind him. For the first time in most of his adolescent and all of his adult life, he was at peace with the world he had known. Only Ida Edwards knew of an immediate preliminary plan. She had wanted to be with him. "No, kid," he said, "you stay home. I'll be back in two days." Gay in spirit and vibrantly healthy, he boarded a train without telling anyone else where he was going.

"But when I come back," he whispered waggishly into Mr. Albacker's ear, "I'll be beautiful again and everybody'll be saying, 'Look, there goes Barrymore!'"

Three days later, October 22, 1926, he was dead in an Atlantic City hospital, the result of haemorrhages following an operation on the nose it had taken a million punches to misshape.

"I haven't took a drink since that day" Mr. Albacker said, "and I never will."

We were standing at Greb's grave one midnight last September in Pittsburgh's Calvary Cemetery, spotlighted by an enormous harvest moon. It wasn't as glaring as the klieg lights under which we had seen him so many times and in so many places - in the great cities, in the smaller ones and at whistle stops in between. There weren't any boos or cheers, either, but only the flipping of our ties in the autumn breeze. Into Mr. Albacker's memory hurtled minutiae of the rough road our pilgrim had travelled - the time in London when, after listening to instructions by the referee and shaking the hand of his opponent in the Inter-Allied bouts following the first world war, Sailor Greb's itchy hand continued on up to the chin and won him one of the quickest knockouts in ring history; a hellish twenty-rounder in Cumberland when he smashed Jackie Clarke into a wooden ring post, the crash collapsing part of the ring which had to be held up the rest of the fight by club flunkies; in New York the night he came from behind to crucify Mickey Walker with such breathless speed that a spectator said Greb's movements reminded him of a humming bird with a stallion's power; all those bruising Tunney fights which one writer summed up as..."the most vicious since the Romans fought with cestuses"; that gruelling, hateful fight in Pittsburgh with the rain bouncing off the canvas like rubber balls, lightning splashing, thunder rolling, and Greb's fury mounting as he slashed a brave but overmatched Tommy Gibbons into unquestionable defeat; the night in Child's restaurant in Atlantic City when four thugs strode menacingly toward Mr. Albacker, whose back was turned. Greb hit them so hard and so suddenly it panicked them into dropping their weapons on the floor and pleading for mercy; the time—

"Hap," I interrupted, "it's a little eerie up here."

"Don't be afraid, Jim," he said. "Harry won't let nobody hurt you."

THE END